VICTORIAN PARTY-GIVING
ON EVERY SCALE

VICTORIAN PARTY-GIVING

ON EVERY SCALE

NONSUCH

First published 1880
Copyright © in this edition Nonsuch Publishing Limited, 2007

Nonsuch Publishing Limited
Cirencester Road, Chalford, Stroud, Gloucestershire, GL6 8PE, UK
www.nonsuch-publishing.com

Nonsuch Publishing is an imprint of NPI Media Group Limited

British Library Cataloguing in Publication Data
A catalogue record for this book is available from the British Library

ISBN 978 1 84588 369 0

Typesetting and origination by Nonsuch Publishing Limited
Printed and bound in Great Britain by Oaklands Book Services Limited

CONTENTS

INTRODUCTION TO THE MODERN EDITION

D URING THE NINETEENTH CENTURY A new type of literature became popular amongst the middle and upper classes of Victorian society: the social instruction manual. This genre was widely read by women in particular, as it provided for them a wealth of advice upon all manner of subjects, ranging from household management to etiquette and manners. The sheer volume of guidance that appeared during this period indicates the level of demand for this kind of social and domestic instruction. Indeed, by the end of the century this type of book was considered an essential tool for any woman who had a home to run, with volumes such as *Mrs Beeton's Book of Household Management,* whose name became synonymous with domesticity and cookery, being one of the most popular and enduring of its type.

Manuals like this offered detailed, systematic advice on matters such as the management of domestic staff, the proper methods of dining and how to attain the correct manners for good society. The popularity they attained can be accounted for by the strict rules of etiquette that prevailed in Victorian society, which, if flouted, could lead to gossip or even social exclusion. It was, therefore, considered vitally important to portray an image of conventionality; following the correct rules for entertaining, for example, was one way to achieve this. *Party-Giving on Every Scale*, published anonymously in 1880, provided a rule-book for those faced with the 'pleasant yet onerous task of entertaining'. It offered tips on how successfully to organise every class of popular entertainment, from simple luncheons to grand balls, in a style that was in keeping with the latest fashions in Victorian society. These considerations were viewed with importance by women simply because their roles were almost completely limited to those within the domestic sphere, which meant that perfecting the art of hospitality was viewed as one of the few ways in which they could demonstrate their abilities, and be rewarded for this with social prestige and status. Many women, upon marriage, would also look to these books for practical guidance on their new role as a housewife, which often required skills of which they would have had little previous experience. The underlying motive for wishing to get these things right was due to the common perception of what was seen as correct, acceptable behaviour. The emergence of the middle classes meant there was an even greater need for reassurance on matters such as etiquette, especially for the entertaining of guests, during which the household and servants would be on display.

Books such as *Party-Giving on Every Scale* exemplify the particularly strict rules that existed at this time relating to the 'proper' methods of dining. This was due to the great importance of the dinner party as a social function within Victorian society. The provision of hospitality had by this time evolved from the act of moral duty it had been in early modern times into a competitive domestic entertainment which served as a symbol of prestige. It had essentially become an aspirational tool through which the host could display his household means and endeavour to improve the family's social connections. Every tiny detail, from the food which was served and how it was presented to the way it was eaten, were all considered indicators of wealth and status, or at the very least the status that the host aspired to. The dining room thus became the most important room in the Victorian home, as this was where the family represented itself to the outside world. The common dining practices that were followed to these ends gradually became standardised into a strict code, and therein lay the need for instruction manuals which could be consulted to ensure that every last detail of the code was followed. Books such as *Cassells Household Guide* are typical of the type of manual which would have been referred to for advice, and most of them were remarkably uniform in content, supplying 'trustworthy' advice covering the 'customs in most general use throughout England', which, if followed, would remove any 'embarrassing doubts' about dinner-giving practices.

The giving of hospitality had an important status in Victorian society, and was considered to have the ability to help people to gain a greater footing in society. It is certainly no surprise that guide books upon this subject suddenly abounded during the period, if indeed so much was dependant upon navigating oneself successfully through a dinner party. This importance attached to entertaining will of course strike the modern reader as disproportionate, as it now neither holds the same significance nor requires adherence to such strict rules. However, books such as *Party-Giving on Every Scale* can still offer useful tips today, as well as shedding light on the social history of Victorian England and providing a fascinating insight into a literary genre which was so popular at this time.

PREFACE

IN CONSEQUENCE OF THE FAVOUR with which the three former Works have been received by the public at large, a fourth is now placed before it in the hope that it will merit the kind appreciation which has been so freely awarded to its predecessors.

A word of thanks must be here given to those members of the Press who have given such valuable support and found so much to praise and approve of in the volumes already alluded to; whilst to those reviewers who have amused themselves solely by levelling chaff at the *nom de plume* of the Author, we can only say, in the language of the poet—

Charge, Chester, charge! On, Stanley, on!

INTRODUCTORY REMARKS

Entertaining guests, either on a large or a small scale, enters more or less into the social life of most heads of families; and whatever the number of guests entertained, or whatever direction the entertainment may take, whether a dinner of four, or a ball of four hundred, or an amateur performance with an audience of fifty, or a concert with an audience of two hundred, each and all demand an outlay of money in a greater or lesser degree; and outside the question of expense is the equally important one of the actual and practical knowledge necessary for arranging and organizing entertainments of any kind. These may prove either great successes or great failures—according to the tact and judgment displayed; and although no doubt much depends upon individual skill and good sense, yet to those inexperienced in the matter of entertaining guests, certain leading rules, suggestions, and statistics cannot fail to be of service; and obviate many incongruities, mistakes, or *fiascos,* which might otherwise arise, more especially in the catering department. The expenses attendant upon large entertainments have grown so heavy, from force of example, that those possessing moderate means, but hospitable proclivities, feel themselves debarred from entering the ranks of entertainers through being unable to follow in the wake of more wealthy individuals. Therefore as they cannot afford to do things well in the orthodox and conventional style, they think it best to do nothing at all in the way of hospitality; thus many pleasant social gatherings are sacrificed at the shrine of custom, fashion, and expense. In the present work the details relating to every class of entertainment, from the most economical to the most expensive, have been carefully gone into, not from a theoretical point of view, but gathered from years of experience and tables of figures, the strongest of facts upon which to work. Beginners in the pleasant yet onerous task of entertaining—young married people, for instance, or those who have come into money, or mothers who commence entertaining on bringing out their daughters—will find the present little work of valuable assistance, and even old practised hands will, we trust, see herein much to approve of and many suggestions worthy of consideration.

Part I

I

WEDDING BREAKFASTS

Wedding Breakfasts on various scales of Expense—Sitting-down Breakfasts—Standing-up Breakfasts—Arrangements for Wedding Breakfasts—What is given at Large Breakfasts—At Small Breakfasts—Expensive dishes—Inexpensive dishes—Wedding cakes—Various sizes and cost—Wines usually given—Average quantities drunk by a given number of Guests.

THE ORTHODOX "WEDDING BREAKFAST" MIGHT more properly be termed a "Wedding Luncheon," as it assumes the character of that meal to a great extent; in any case, it bears little relation to the breakfast of the day, although the title of breakfast is still applied to it, out of compliment to tradition. As recently as fifty years ago luncheon was not a recognised meal even in the wealthiest families, and the marriage feast was modernised into the wedding breakfast, which appellation this entertainment still bears.

The difference between a small wedding breakfast and a large one is rather in the number and variety of the dishes provided than in the character of the said viands; while with regard to the display made of plate, fruit, and flowers, this is necessarily regulated by the style of breakfast given and the number of guests invited. There are many reasons besides economy which decide a small breakfast being given in preference to a large one; first and foremost, the wishes of the bridegroom. Bridegrooms, as a rule, would gladly dispense as far as possible with what they term parade or fuss. This reasonable wish is too often overruled by the bride and the female members of her family. When the mother of a bride opposes the request for a quiet wedding on the part of her future son-in-law, she does so from politic reasons. It is the rule, she knows, to invite all those who have sent presents to the bride, and she does not wish to appear wanting in hospitality towards her friends.

A recent family bereavement is an all-sufficient reason for giving a very small breakfast, and for limiting the invitations to the immediate relatives of both families, or for dispensing with the breakfast altogether. Ill-health on the part of the bride's parents is an equally good reason for a breakfast not being given. Again, people who reside in the country often find it expedient to be married in town, either from an hotel or from furnished apartments; if from the former, the hotel charge for the breakfast is one guinea per head, including wine; if from the latter, a confectioner's charge is 15s. to one guinea per head, *not* including wine, for which an extra charge is made of from 4s. 6d. to 5s. per head. If the wine is supplied by a wine merchant instead of by the confectioner, the cost is according to the number of dozen ordered, or rather to the quantity actually drunk by the guests.

A breakfast given at an hotel or one given in furnished apartments offers little choice in the arrangements, as in either case there is but one alternative, the hotel *cuisine* or the confectioner's *cuisine*, neither of which ranks particularly high in public estimation or public favour in comparison with the home *cuisine*. When a breakfast is given at the home of a bride and is not "sent in" or supplied by a confectioner, but "made at home," it is considered a very superior style of breakfast, in other words, a more fashionable one to give. But this is taking for granted that the home cook is equal to the occasion, or that the services of an experienced cook can be secured for the event. We say fashionable, because in those houses where a superior cook is kept, whether a man or woman cook, French or English, it is usual to have everything made at home, and it fellows as a matter of course that everything home-made by such experienced hands is decidedly preferable to things made to order at a pastry cook's, the reason for this doubtless being that in the home kitchen there is no stint in quantities and qualities, and the best and freshest of materials are procured, and as no profit is to accrue, the one object is to provide the best of its kind that can be compassed, whether it be of fish, flesh, fowl, or fruit, and although the credit of a confectioner is at stake in giving satisfaction, he yet cannot afford to be as liberal with his materials as can the home cook, and therefore the look of a dish is more studied by confectioners than its taste, freshness, flavour, or quality, and providing the chickens are tied with coloured ribbons, one cannot expect to find them over young or over tender, and we doubt if the lobster salad has much improved since the days when a popular writer and *bon vivant* declared that the distinctive mark between a home-made and a confectioner's salad was, that the one had lobster in it and the other had not.

Next to the question of undeniable superiority ranks the question of economy, and a very large saving is effected in having things made at home, but when a cook is not skilful enough to undertake smart-looking sweets, or when the kitchen appliances do not admit of an extra amount of cooking being done, it is advisable to have the plain and substantial dishes made at home, and to rely upon the aid of a confectioner to furnish the lighter portion of the breakfast, and submit to the inevitable and make the best of the compromise.

When the giver of a wedding breakfast has a country house, a home farm, and home preserves, a well-stocked kitchen garden, hothouses, and a fine conservatory, it is merely a question of making use of produce ready to hand, whether the breakfast be given in town or country, and the cost of a breakfast under such conditions may be estimated at 15 per cent. less than if supplied from town shops at town prices but it is the few and not the many who are thus happily situated, and it is to the latter only that the statistics contained in this little work apply.

In regulating the quantities required for a wedding breakfast, it must be borne in mind that each dish should be provided in proportion to the number and variety of the dishes given, and not in accordance with the number of guests invited. This is the point where an inexperienced housekeeper often makes a mistake in providing sufficient of each dish for the total number of guests, thus incurring a most unnecessary expense and a needlessly lavish display of food without a corresponding amount of variety.

The true art of giving a wedding breakfast is to introduce as much variety into the *menu* as possible, and to tempt the appetite with light and *appétissant* delicacies, rather than to repel it by the display of a huge quantity of heavy and substantial fare.

There are many conventional and, we might say, traditional delicacies which it is thought incumbent to provide for a fashionable wedding breakfast, and heading the list of these is the richly ornamented wedding cake. It was formerly the custom to send a slice of wedding cake to every friend or acquaintance of the bride and bridegroom, and this custom naturally demanded that the wedding cake should be as large as the circle of friends was wide, thus a cake weighing perhaps ninety pounds was often a necessary appendage to the wedding breakfast, but as this custom is now obsolete, and it is neither considered "good taste" to send slices of wedding cake to friends, nor to offer it on the occasion of bridal visits being received, it is altogether unnecessary to keep up the size of the cake, as it is an expensive and indigestible compound, a little of which goes a very long way; the quantity of wedding cake cut for, if not eaten by, say a hundred wedding guests would not average more than 12 lbs., therefore a cake weighing 20 lbs. would be large enough even for this number of guests, leaving a wide margin wherewith to satisfy the demands of the household and the children of the family, who are in reality the most appreciative consumers of this unwholesome dainty. A cake of large dimensions is still required, however, at a country wedding, when the bride's father is the owner of broad acres, and has many tenants and dependents, the ladies of whose families look for the regulation piece of wedding cake to put under their pillows that they may dream of their future husbands; but for the generality of wedding breakfasts, a cake weighing 20 lbs. would meet all requirements.

The usual charge for wedding cake at a confectioner's is from 3s. to 4s. per lb., according to the amount of ornamentation indulged in; this quality of cake can be made at home for say 1s. 6d. per lb., and every description of ornament can be bought separately wherewith to decorate it after the iceing process has been completed. But as a wedding cake is provided more from custom and for the look of the thing than for any other reason, there is no particular advantage to the guests in its being made at home, and as the saving made in the expense of the cake entails no little anxiety and responsibility upon the cook, unless she is a proficient in the art of cake making, iceing, and ornamenting, etc., it is unwise to incur the risk of a failure where so large an amount of material is concerned, although, to a judge of cake, one made by an experienced hand at home is a far more enjoyable *morceau* than one purchased at a pastry cook's or cake manufactory. Some ladies have an idea that the wedding cake should assume the proportions of a trophy on the breakfast table, constructed of a pyramid of sugar, plaster of Paris, artificial orange-blossoms, true lovers'-knots, Cupids, and miniature bannerets, shields, crests, and monograms; but this elaborate style of ornamentation is not in the best possible taste, and a neater and less ornate class of cake decoration is considered more fashionable—and there is fashion even in wedding cakes.

The newest and most approved style of wedding breakfast, is to combine in a judicious manner both hot and cold viands, hot and cold roasts, and the regulation cold sweets.

Soup is not given at wedding breakfasts at smart and fashionable houses, it is only provided when the confectioner has the management of the breakfast, when two soups generally head the *menu*.

Oysters are now occasionally given at wedding breakfasts; it is rather unusual to do so on account of the expense, and also because young ladies are not given to eating oysters, but oysters are a *bonne bouche* always appreciated by men when provided; for a party of fifty guests, fourteen dozen oysters would be an average number to supply, the cost of which would be 3s. per dozen.

To enumerate every dish and delicacy that is or ought to be given at a wedding breakfast would demand more space than is here at command; but in the following pages will be found the most popular and appropriate things to provide for an entertainment of this description. Cold salmon is one of the most popular dishes to give, served whole or as *tranche de saumon*, garnished with cucumber, or as a mayonnaise. For a party of fifty people, 14 to 15 lbs. would be sufficient. The cost of salmon usually ranges from 2s. to 4s. 6d.; it is seldom as low as 1s. 6d., although in July a fairly good salmon may be bought at that price; but like everything else it ceases to become a delicacy when its low price makes it common fare. It reaches its highest price, perhaps, during January and February. (See Chapter XI, "The Cost of Dinners.")

For the above quantity of salmon four cucumbers at from 9d. to 1s. each would be required, whether served with the cold salmon, or as a garniture to the dishes of *tranche de saumon*.

Salmon to be enjoyable should look fresh and be of a tempting pink colour, but it not unfrequently happens that salmon "sent in" ready cooked and dressed, presents such a pallid colourless appearance that it is not easily recognised as salmon, and one is led to inquire what it is; it proves as unpleasing to the palate as to the eye, being dry, hard, and flavourless. Salmon that has been some time on ice presents this appearance when cooked, and hence the necessity of guarding against its not being perfectly fresh.

One hot *entrée* is always considered sufficient for a wedding breakfast; this invariably takes the form of mutton or lamb cutlets, according to the season of the year. For a party of fifty people four dishes of cutlets would be required, each dish containing from 12 to 14 small cutlets. Cutlets are an exception to the rule before laid down, and are provided in accordance with the number of guests present. Eighteen pounds of neck of lamb or mutton would be requisite for this number of cutlets, the cost of which, if lamb, would range from 1s. to 1s. 2d. per lb., and if of mutton, from 11d. to 1s. per lb.; thus this quantity of lamb cutlets would in March, when the neck of lamb is charged at 1s. 2d. per lb., amount to 21s., and in June the same quantity would amount to 18s.; when lamb is at 1s. per lb., the same quantity of mutton cutlets would cost 16s. 6d. or 18s., according to whether mutton was at 11d. or 1s. per lb. If the cutlets are served without a vegetable, 3s. would be sufficient for cooking ingredients and sauce; if served with either cucumber, peas, asparagus points, or spinach, 5s. must be allowed, and 1s. for ingredients. Lobster mayonnaise, or *mayonnaise de Homard*, is as much a standing dish at a wedding breakfast as is the wedding cake; if well made it is a very good thing, if badly made it is about the worst thing that can be given. For a party of fifty people, four dishes of lobster mayonnaise would be a fair proportion. Four full-sized dishes would cost, on the average, 5s. 6d. to 7s. per dish. Aspic of lobster is also a good dish to give, the cost being the same as a lobster mayonnaise. Lobster salad is less expensive than a lobster mayonnaise, less lobster and less cream being required in its composition. Thus a full-sized dish of lobster salad could be made for 4s.

Suprême de volaille à la crême is one of those dishes which are very much seen, if not very much liked, at wedding breakfasts; a full-sized dish could be made at 5s. 6d. and even a trifle cheaper when chickens are bought by the half-dozen. For a party of fifty people, four dishes of *suprême de volaille* would be required.

Galantine of chicken or *galantine de poularde* is often given; the cost of four fair-sized dishes would average one guinea. Plover's eggs, *œufs de pluviers*, with aspic jelly, or *en croustade*, is a favourite delicacy at all times, more especially at a wedding breakfast. The cost of plover's eggs varies from 2s. 6d. to 7s. per doz. during the time they are in season. For a party of fifty people five dozen plover's eggs would be required, and 3s. must be allowed for stock, &c., for making aspic jelly. Prawns in aspic jelly make a pretty dish, twelve dozen prawns at 1s. per dozen would be a fair proportion to provide.

Collared eel with aspic jelly is another tasty *chaudfroid*; the cost of this also depends upon the price of eels per pound, which usually averages from 10d. to 1s. 6d. per lb.; 6 lbs. of eels would make two full-sized dishes.

Petits pâtés de foie gras are given more or less, but they are expensive in their way, and are not eaten by the majority of guests, that is to say, by young ladies, therefore five-and-twenty of these *pâtés* would be sufficient to provide for a party of fifty guests at a wedding breakfast. A *pâté de foie gras* at 15s. would be sufficient to make this number of *pâtés*.

Pâtés de Gibier garnie à l'aspic is another frivolous dish, and is made of pounded game and served with aspic jelly; the cost of game, &c., for making fifty *pâtés* would average 8s.

Petits pâtés à la Financière, being made of chicken, would cost a little less, say 5s. for fifty *pâtés*.

Quenelles of chicken with truffles are also given. The proportion for a party of fifty people could be made for 12s., and would average four fair-sized dishes.

Cold cutlets *à la Macédoine*, or with aspic jelly, are often given, two dishes of this cold *entrée* would be sufficient to provide, amongst other *entrées*, for the before-mentioned number of guests, and allowing twelve cutlets to each dish, if of lamb, they could be made at 5s. a dish, or of mutton at 4s., allowing 8 lbs. of either lamb or mutton for four-and-twenty cutlets.

A *chaudfroid* of partridges with aspic jelly is a smart but rather an expensive dish to give, the cost of which depends upon the market price; if 4s. a brace, the cost of two fair-sized dishes containing twenty-four cutlets or fillets would amount to 15s., allowing three brace of partridges at 4s. a brace, and 3s. for ingredients.

Quails *farcies*, or *en croustade*, is another smart-looking dish, the cost of which also depends upon the market price, usually ranging from 12s. to 18s. per doz.; two dozen quails would be a fair proportion to order for this given number of guests.

In ordering a wedding breakfast, it should always be taken into consideration that certain *chaudfroids* are not generally eaten by ladies, it is therefore an unnecessary expense to provide for more than one-third of the number of guests present.

Mauviettes farcie, or a *chaudfroid* of larks, is another *récherché* dish to give, and ranges from 1s. 6d. to 3s. per dozen; three dozen larks would be a fair proportion to order; 2s. 6d. to 3s. must be allowed for truffles and other ingredients.

There are numerous other *chaudfroids* which could be introduced with advantage at a wedding breakfast, similar as regards cost to these already given, which offer a still wider choice in arranging a *menu*. After the *chaudfroids* the *grosses pièces* are next to be considered.

The *grosses pièces* given at a wedding breakfast are invariably cold, with the exception of hot roast chickens, but these are only occasionally given; again, in the game season it is thought fashionable to give hot roast pheasants or hot roast partridges, but this also is the exception and not the rule, as, though the cost of game and poultry is the same, whether served hot or cold, yet the former entails an additional amount of trouble.

Chickens are given all the year round, and a good judge of poultry selects Surrey fowls in preference to any other in the market for roasting.

The price of these chickens ranges from 4s. to 6s. each, and the price of capons from 7s. to 12s. each. For *chaudfroids* of chicken, Sussex and Boston fowls answer the purpose very well, and are a trifle cheaper; they average from 2s. 6d. to 5s. 6d. each.

Roast chicken is garnished in a variety of ways, as for instance:—

Poulets rôtis au cressons—Sauce Tartare—À la Bechamel, etc., etc. For a party of fifty people four roast chickens would be a fair proportion, and including sauce ingredients the cost of these would be one guinea, allowing 8s. a couple for the chickens. Roast pheasants are given when in season, and the same number of pheasants would be provided at the same cost.

Roast turkey, or as it is termed *Dinde farcie aux truffles*, is a popular *grosse pièce*.

A turkey weighing 14 lbs. would be an average-sized one for a party of fifty people; the cost of which would amount to one guinea, including tongue, truffles, and other ingredients.

Glazed tongue with aspic jelly is a ubiquitous dish at wedding breakfasts. Two tongues, weighing 6 lbs. each, would be provided for a party of fifty people; the cost of which, including aspic jelly, and glaze, would amount to 7s. 6d. each. Cold ham is always provided, although but little eaten at a wedding breakfast, the other dishes being more attractive to appetites in general. A ham weighing 16 lbs. is an average size to give. Westphalia hams have a fine flavour, but are not so generally given as are York hams.

The best mode of cooking hams, rendering them additionally tender, will be found described in the Chapter on Breakfasts.

A large cold game-pie is generally given when game is in season; the cost of one weighing 16 lbs. would amount to one guinea, if made at home. When lamb is in season a fore-quarter of lamb is often given amongst the other cold things; the price varying from 1s. to 1s. 4d. per lb., according to the season of the year, and also as to whether it is house lamb. Pigeon-pie is sometimes given when game is not in season; the price of pigeons ranges from 10d. to 1s. 6d. each; two average-sized pies would be provided for a party of fifty.

Meat-pies and patties made of ham and veal, or beef, are not given at wedding breakfasts; cold patty is not appreciated by the many.

Galantine de veau and glazed beef are equally unacceptable, and are only resorted to by those who have a poor imagination and cannot think of anything better to provide.

Sandwiches made of potted game or potted fish find a place on every wedding breakfast-table; pounded game, lobster, anchovy, *foie gras*, all make excellent sandwiches, and the cost of either of these may be estimated at from 3s. to 4s. per dozen. Six dishes of sandwiches would be an average number to provide.

Smart looking sweets are always a feature at a wedding breakfast, "jellies" taking first rank of these. *Macédoine* jelly is the most popular; the cost of which, when home made, amounts to 3s. 6d. per quart mould.

Jellies flavoured with liqueur, either Noyeau or Maraschino, are much given; when made at home the cost of these amounts to 2s. 6d. per ½ pint mould. Jellies flavoured with either strawberry, raspberry, cherry, lemon, or currant, are not *à la mode*.

From four to six jellies would be provided for a party of fifty; for further details on this head, see Chapter V, "Balls and Dances."

Creams, although not so generally eaten as are jellies, have yet a popularity of their own. There are numerous creams to be avoided as being unpalatable and unfashionable. The following are those usually given: strawberry cream, raspberry cream, apricot cream, coffee cream, Italian cream, Vanille cream. Two of these creams are always selected for a wedding breakfast, say strawberry and coffee, raspberry and Italian. Four creams would be provided, two of each kind; the cost of these would average 4s. each, if made at home. Meringues, *Meringues glacé*, are much given; they are filled with either of the creams above mentioned; 2½ dozen would be the proportion for a party of fifty, and would cost, if made at home and the cream flavoured with fruit, 4s. per dozen; if purchased, the charge is from 10s. to 12s. per dozen. Smaller meringues, half the size of *meringues glacé*, can be made at 2s. per dozen, and purchased at 4s. per dozen.

It is the custom to give certain descriptions of *Gâteaux*, including *Gâteau Napolitaine, Gâteau Bordeux, Gâteau Bretagne, Gâteau Savoy;* the cost of either of these, made at home, would range from 3s. to 5s.; if ordered at a confectioner's, from 7s. 6d. to 10s. 6d.

Tipsy cake, although looked upon in the light of a second-class sweet, is yet generally eaten when given, and is preferred to the more ornamental and sugary sweets; therefore, in justice, it should take rank amongst first-class sweets. A good sized tipsy cake can be made at home for 5s. with fresh sponge cakes soaked in good sherry and good brandy. A similar size can be bought at a pastry cook's for 10s. 6d. Two *Gâteaux,* or two tipsy cakes, would be the proportion for a party of fifty.

Amongst other sweets given at wedding breakfasts are, *Macédoine de Fruits, Suprême de Fruits, Chartreuse de Fruits, Crême Plombieres Glacé*, &c., which are neither more nor less than moulds of pressed fruits made either of one kind of fruit, or of many kinds of fruit, with or without cream. The cost of these would average from 3s. to 5s., according to the fruit used and to the season of the year. If made of strawberries or raspberries when well in season, four dishes would be given; if more expensive fruit, such as apricots or peaches, were used, two dishes would be sufficient where expense is studied. *Nougat à la Chantilly, Les Génoises Glaces au Noyeau, Les Puits-d'amour Glaces au Chocolate,* are pretty looking sweets to give, and are always known by their French names even when made by an English cook, and are here given that they may be employed in making out a *menu*.

Ornamental pastry is given, although but little eaten. The cost of this pastry ranges from 6d. to 8d. per dozen if made at home, and is. to 2s. per dozen if bought.

It is not usual to give ices at a wedding breakfast, the majority of guests not being inclined to indulge in them thus early in the day.

Hothouse fruit is given either in a large or small quantity, according to inclination, although a certain quantity is, as a rule, provided.

Grapes at a guinea per pound, a pineapple at from one guinea to 25s., peaches at 2s. each, run into money, as do forced strawberries; therefore, unless money or fruit is plentiful, little or no fruit need be given.

When pineapple is given, two average-sized ones at from 10s. 6d. to 12s. 6d. each, or one large one at 25s., would be sufficient.

Four dishes of grapes would be required, containing 2 lbs. each, the cost of which would be regulated according to the season of the year, varying from 3s 6d. to one guinea per lb.

Forced strawberries are seldom given at wedding breakfasts, unless luxury reigns paramount, when there is no saying to what extent a giver of a wedding feast may be tempted to go; but with ordinary means strawberries would only be given when they were at a reasonable price, as everyone eats them, generally speaking. From four to six dishes of strawberries would be required for a party of fifty, the cost of which would average from 2s. to 5s. per lb., allowing 1 lb. to a dish.

The fruit provided at a wedding breakfast is given by way of dessert, and the fruit in season is always selected for the purpose, thus melons, pears, peaches, apricots, are given in their turn, the cost of which is determined by the market price.

With regard to the wines given at a wedding breakfast, champagne, sherry and claret are those most usually drunk, and champagne far more so than either sherry or claret, thus for a party of fifty, the proportion of champagne drunk would probably average twenty-one bottles, allowing half-a-bottle to each man to the number of five-and-twenty, and one bottle to three ladies to the number of five-and-twenty.

Thus for a party of fifty guests, two dozen of champagne would be sufficient to provide, leaving three bottles in reserve, computing at the rate of six glasses to the bottle. The cost of champagne would range from 60s. per dozen upwards.

In addition to this quantity of champagne, seven-and-a-half bottles of sherry would probably be drunk, allowing one bottle to five men, and one bottle to ten ladies, at the rate of ten glasses to the bottle. Although this quantity would only be drunk, yet for a party of fifty it would he necessary to give out ten bottles of sherry for the purpose of filling the decanters. The cost of sherry usually drunk at wedding breakfasts varies from 36s. to 60s. per dozen.

As claret is now very much drunk, decanters of claret would also be provided; six would be sufficient, each containing one bottle of claret. The usual cost of claret given ranges from 36s. to 66s. per dozen.

Liqueurs are generally given with coffee, that is to say, Brandy, Orange Brandy, Curaçao, Chartreuse, &c.

Soda-water and seltzer-water would also be provided, and one dozen and a half at 3s. per dozen would be sufficient for this number of guests.

The arrangements for a wedding breakfast rather depend upon whether it is a sitting-down or standing-up one.

This is ruled in a great measure by the amount of space at command, and the number of guests invited and number of the acceptances received.

Either mode of giving a wedding breakfast is equally fashionable, but oftener than not the two modes are combined in one, and small round tables are arranged at one end of the dining-room for a sit-down breakfast, and a long buffet is arranged at the other for a stand-up breakfast. (See "Manners and Tone of Good Society.")

A larger number of guests can be accommodated at a standing-up breakfast than at a sitting-down one, it is besides less expensive in many ways. Hot *entrées* and hot roasts are then not given, and the cold *entrées* and sweets are less elaborate, and in consequence less expensive; and as it is the custom at standing-up breakfasts for gentlemen to help the ladies and themselves to what they require, it follows that fewer waiters are needed for the occasion. For one thing, champagne is not handed to the guests in rotation, but is asked for as it is wanted; and it is the province, privilege, pleasure, or whatever he may please to consider it, of each gentleman who takes a lady down to breakfast to ask for champagne for her of the servants in attendance; and to see that it is quickly brought.

Soup is only given when the breakfast is entirely a sitting-down one, and it is more usual not to give it than to give it.

The usual width of a table or tables for a wedding breakfast is from 3 feet to 3 feet 6 inches; the manner of placing the tables depends upon the size of the room and the number of guests expected.

A sitting-down breakfast demands more space than does a standing-up one; for the former 18 inches would be allowed for each guest, for the later 12 inches could be made to suffice; and small round tables are more convenient for sitting-down breakfasts than are long tables.

An ordinary telescope dining-table, averaging from 4 feet 6 inches to 5 feet in width, extended to the required length, is brought into requisition when the guests do not exceed fifty in number, as thirty people could well be seated at a full-sized table, and the remaining twenty be accommodated at three or four small round tables.

If the resources of the house cannot furnish the requisite number of chairs, the deficiency is made up with hired chairs; the cost of hire of cane chairs ranges from 4s. 6d. to 6s. per dozen.

When extra table linen is required for a large sitting-down wedding breakfast, the cost of hire of *serviettes* is 2s. per dozen, and of table-cloths 6d. per yard.

Flowers and fruit occupy the centre of the table, and with regard to both flowers and fruit, very little, or very much, may be spent upon them. Cut flowers, ferns, grasses and moss are the most fashionable style of table decoration, and are preferred to tall plants.

A table decorated in the spring with primroses, violets, or lilies of the valley, or in the summer with roses, has a better effect than if decorated with a variety of flowers. The cost of these is regulated by the severity or mildness of the season.

The wedding-cake is placed in the centre of the long table or *buffet*, and the dishes containing the various cold *entrées*, *grosses pièces,* and sweets are placed the length of the table, on both sides, and are arranged according to the extent of the *menu,* allowing an equal number for each side. Four decanters of sherry and the same of claret are also placed on each side of the table.

The usual cover consists of two large knives, two large forks, a glass for sherry, a glass for champagne, and a claret glass. *Serviettes* are only provided at sitting-down breakfasts.

At a standing-up breakfast the cover would only include one knife and one large fork, and neither table-spoon, *serviette*, nor roll would be given. A second-sized dinner-plate is placed between each knife and fork. Rolls are handed in a basket, and a clean fork and dessert-spoon are handed as required. At a standing-up breakfast space does not admit of more than two glasses being given to each cover, and champagne and sherry glasses only are included in the cover.

Dozens of knives and forks, plates and glasses, are arranged on a side-table, to be handed to the guests when required. As an extra number of knives, forks, plates and glasses are invariably required in addition to the resources of a household, the requisite articles are hired at so much per dozen. Plates, 1s. per dozen; Dessert-plates, 1s. 6d. to 2s. per dozen; Dishes of all sizes from 2s. to 4s. per dozen; Champagne-glasses, 1s. per dozen; Glasses for Sherry, 9d. per dozen; Tumblers, 9d. per dozen; Large Knives, 2s. 6d. per dozen; Large Forks, 2s. per dozen; Small Forks, 1s. 6d. per dozen; Table-spoons, 2s. per dozen; Dessert-spoons, 1s. 6d. per dozen. Cups and Saucers, for either tea or coffee, 1s. 6d. per dozen; Tea-

spoons, 1s. 6d. per dozen. The charge for the hire of a cake-stand
depends upon the size of the cake, and ranges from 2s. 6d. to 15s.
and everything requisite for serving a wedding breakfast in the
way of china, plate and glass can be hired at a moderate cost at
any well-known establishment.

The waiting required at a wedding breakfast being comparatively
slight, five men servants would be a fair proportion for a sitting-
down breakfast of fifty guests, their duty being simply to hand
round the hot *entrée* and hot roast, if one is given, to supply
clean plates and forks to the guests, and to open and hand the
champagne.

With the exception of the before-mentioned hot *entrée*, all
the dishes included in the menu are placed upon the table, and
the guests help themselves in place of the dishes being handed
round by the servants. The *menu* for a wedding breakfast is
arranged on the following scale, whether the guests number
25 or 100, the difference being in the quantities provided in
proportion to the number of the guests, and not in an increased
variety of dishes.

The breakfast commences with one hot *entrée*, if the breakfast
is a sitting-down one; it is also fashionable, although not
obligatory, to give one hot roast in addition to a hot *entrée*, at a
sitting-down breakfast.

At a standing-up breakfast soup is never given; neither are hot
entrées or hot roasts provided.

The following men are given as a general indication of the two
classes of wedding breakfasts usually given. When one hot *entrée*
is given, two or three cold *entrées* would be provided, three to five
grosses pièces, and six to eight *entremets,* including those of fish and
game, in addition to the sweets coming under this head.

MENU

Entrée Chaude

Côtelettes d'Agneau aux petits Pois

Grosses Pièces

Quartier d'Agneau rôti   Poulets rôtis
        Jambon de York   Langues de Boeuf
            Pâté de Fois-gras

Entrées Froides

Tranches de Salmon aux Concombres   Mayonnaise de Homard
    Oeufs de Pluviers en aspic   Mauviettes à la Lucullus
        Salades à la Russe   Sandwiches Régence

Entremets

Gelée à la Macédoine   Gelée au Maraschino
    Gâteau Napolitaine   Meringues Glacé à la Crême
            Chartreuses de Fruit
        Crême à l'Italienne   Crême de Café
            Pâtisseries variés   Glaces

MENU

Entrée Chaude

Côtelettes de Mouton piquées en Chevreuil

Grosses Pièces

Dinde farcie aux Truffles   Jambon de York
Poulets rôtis   Langue de Boeuf

Entrées Froides

Mayonnaise de Saumon   Salade de Homard
Galantine de Poulardes   Aspics de Filets de Soles
Sandwiches Anchovie

Entremets

Gâteau de Bordeaux
Gelée à la Noyeau   Gelée à la Dantzic
Crême de Framboises   Crême à la Vanille
Macédoine de Fruits   Pâtisseries   Glaces

MENU

Faisans rôtis   Pâté de Gibier
Jambon de York   Langue de Boeuf   Poulets rôtis
Poulets à la Bechamel   Chaudfroid d'Anguille en aspic
Salades de Homard   Sandwiches de Gibier
Sandwiches Anchovie   Mayonnaise de Poulets
Jambon découpé en l'aspic
Langue de Boeuf, découpé en aspic

Gelée Noyeau   Gelée Marascino
Trifle à l'Anglaise   Gâteau à la Suisse
Crême Café   Crême de Fraises
Glaces

II

AFTERNOON DANCES

Afternoon Dances—General arrangements—Music—Refreshments—Quantities of Tea, Coffee, Ices, Fruit, &c., for given numbers, and cost in detail of everything requisite in giving large or small dances

A FTERNOON DANCES ARE SELDOM GIVEN in London, but are a popular form of entertainment in the suburbs, in garrison towns, watering-places, etc. In the country an afternoon dance is occasionally preceded by a garden party (see Chapter on "Garden Parties"). An afternoon dance is an inexpensive entertainment; it takes place from four to seven, thus only light refreshments are required, and the heavy expenses of a ball, supper, and long wine bill are not incurred, in addition to many other outlays in the matter of lighting, floral decorations, and the like, to say nothing of the trouble saved, and the inconvenience avoided, to the inmates of a house, by the style of preparations required for a dance given in the afternoon in comparison with one given in the evening.

A dancing cloth strained over the drawing-room carpet is considered preparation enough in the way of a floor for an afternoon dance, and it is seldom thought necessary to have a drawing-room carpet taken up and the floor prepared for dancing. The price of hire of a dancing-cloth is 6s. per square yard, and from one to two guineas per cloth.

An afternoon dance being a sociable and unpretending gathering, at which no display whatever is attempted on the one side or expected on the other, the elders consider it in the light of an "At Home," and the younger portion of the company as an agreeable three hours' dancing, apart from any anxiety on the score of a new ball gown, any simple summery-looking or bright autumn costume being equally appropriate to the occasion.

Afternoon dances would be even more popular than they are, were it not that there is a difficulty in inducing young men to attend them; this is in a measure true of a certain class of men—men over eight-and-twenty, who go to balls and dances as a matter of course, but who dance very little when there. On the other hand, afternoon dances are very popular with the officers of both services; but afternoon dances given by naval officers on board their vessels at various naval stations, and by officers quartered in garrison towns, are on a far larger scale than those given by private individuals. In the one case the expenses of giving a dance are shared by the captain and officers of a ship, or by the colonel and officers of a regiment, which fall lightly upon each officer as compared with the sum he is called upon to pay when a military ball is given to some 600 to 800 guests. These expenses frequently average from £30 to £40 per man, according to the amount spent upon the ball. Married officers, men not too well off, often find these enforced hospitalities a tax upon their pockets, as their share amounts to the same as does that of the chief promoters of these gaieties, the rich young bachelors of the regiment. Thus with the less wealthy officers, small barrack dances, as they are called, are more in favour during the winter season, by way of making some return to the ladies of their acquaintances, than is a grand ball; we say ladies, because men are asked to dine at mess on guest nights, and thus a return of hospitality can be readily offered to them.

At barrack dances, whether given in the afternoon or evening, dancing takes place in the mess-room, refreshments are served by the mess waiters, and prepared in the mess kitchen, the regimental plate decorates the tables, and the string band of the regiment is in attendance, while the decorations of the rooms consisting of military trophies, are the work of the officers' servants, under the superintendence of the officers themselves.

A barrack afternoon dance includes from 80 to 200 guests,

according to the number of dances to be given, and the number of guests to be invited. An afternoon dance on board a ship generally includes from 100 to 250 guests.

The afternoon dances given by ladies include as a rule from 50 to 100 guests, and the preparations for these entertainments are not of an extensive nature, as has already been said. Floral decorations, if attempted at all, are on a very limited scale, and generally comprise vases of cut flowers, in addition to flowering plants, ferns, grasses, &c.; these decorations are not imperative at an afternoon dance, and when indulged in range from 15s. to £15 and upwards.

A piano band is always considered sufficient for these dances, although a string band is occasionally engaged. The cost of either for the three hours would be from 10s. to £1 1s. per man; two performers are considered sufficient by way of a piano band, while the usual sized string band is from nine to twelve performers, see page 69.

The usual refreshments served at afternoon dances are tea and coffee, iced coffee, ices, iced champagne-cup, and claret-cup, fruit, sandwiches, cakes, and biscuits.

The dining-room is used as a tea-room, and the tables are arranged as a buffet at one end of the room. For further description see Chapter III, "Five o'clock Teas." The women servants of the household serve the tea, coffee, and ices, from behind the buffet, one maid servant taking the superintendence of each. The champagne-cup, claret-cup and sherry, are placed on the front of the buffet, and the guests either help themselves or are helped by the men-servants in attendance.

For an afternoon dance of 100 guests the following quantities would be required.

Tea, 5 gallons, allowing 4 ozs. to the gallon. The price and quality of tea greatly depend upon where it is purchased. Some houses sell excellent tea at 2s. per lb., while others charge 3s. per lb. for a tea in no way superior, and for the quantities here given a good tea at 2s. per lb., the quality of which has been tested, would be up to the strength required, otherwise, when making tea by the gallon, it would be advisable to use tea at 2s. 6d. to 3s. per lb.

Coffee, 6 gallons, 4 hot and 2 iced, allowing 8 ozs. of coffee to the gallon, this is supposing the coffee to be first quality.

Cream, 3 pints, at 1s. 6d. or 2s. per pint. If cold milk were given in lieu of cream, 6 pints of milk at 2½d. per pint would be necessary; although cream is sometimes not given by people who are careful of expense, yet when given this outlay is well repaid by the tea being rendered far more palatable.

The milk required to 6 gallons of coffee is 1 quart to the gallon. To this quantity of tea and coffee, 5½ lbs. of sugar would be consumed, at from 4d. to 5d. per lb.; 8 or 9 lbs. would be provided.

Claret-cup: 3 gallons, allowing 4 bottles of claret and 4 bottles of soda-water to the gallon. A fair claret may be bought for this purpose at from 16s. to 24s. per dozen. A lower priced claret of course can be obtained, but such a class of wine is not generally used. The price of soda-water is 1s. 6d. per dozen.

Champagne-cup: 2½ gallons, allowing 4 bottles of champagne and 4 bottles of soda-water to the gallon. Champagne suitable for cup may be bought at 42s. per dozen.

Champagne-cup is only occasionally given, but when given a lesser quantity of claret-cup is provided.

Sherry: 1½ dozen at from 36s. to 48s. per dozen.

Ices: 12 quarts, and the cost of water-ices made at home averages from 1s. 6d. to 2s. per quart, according to the price of the fruit with which they are flavoured, lemon and orange being the least expensive flavour to select. Water-ices purchased at a pastry cook's cost from 5s. to 7s. per quart.

Cream-ices are seldom given at afternoon dances, when expense is studied.

Cream-ices can be made at home in town at 4s. per quart, and the confectioner's charge for the same is from 7s. to 9s. per quart.

Nine dozen wafers would be necessary to 12 quarts of ice. If made at home the cost of these would be 3d. per dozen; if bought at a confectioner's, 6d. per dozen.

Those ladies who wish to give inexpensive afternoon dances, do not pretend to give ices; while those who do not study expense so closely, provide ices as a matter of course.

Fruit is much given during the summer months at these parties—strawberries and cream notably, in addition to hothouse fruit, such as grapes, peaches, pines, &c. This fruit is placed upon the tables in *assiettes montées*, while strawberries and cream are usually served to the guests from a side table at the back of the buffet.

The cost of the fruit is of course regulated by the market price and by the season.

In providing strawberries and cream for 100 guests from 10 lbs. to 12 lbs. would be a fair proportion, and 2½ quarts of cream.

Strawberries and cream is a most popular refreshment to offer at afternoon dances in the strawberry season.

Other fruits such as cherries, raspberries, peaches, grapes, &c., are not provided in any great quantity; two to four dishes of each being the average proportion. The amount of the expense incurred with regard to cakes and biscuits is very optional. A certain quantity of these must of course be provided; but it depends entirely upon the giver of an entertainment whether they consist of smart-looking confectionary, or whether they belong to the genus of the plain and homely; in the one case, pound cake, almond cake, macaroons, ratafias, chocolate *glacé* biscuits, almond *glacé*, &c., would be given, while in the other the most inexpensive class of cake and biscuit would be provided, such as Savoy cake, Madeira cakes, currant cakes, rice cakes, Savoy biscuits, sponge biscuits, &c. Rich pound-cake can be made at home at 1s. per lb.; rich almond cake at 9d. per lb.; Savoy cake at 9d. per lb.; rice cake, 7d. per lb.; currant or plum cake at 8d. per lb.; ratafias and macaroons, 10½d. per lb. Cakes and biscuits made at home are two-thirds less expensive than when purchased ready made.

Eight pounds of cake cut up into small thick pieces would be the proportion, in addition to one or two uncut cakes, and 6 to 8 lbs. of fancy biscuits. Where ices or strawberries and cream are not given, one-fourth more of both cake and biscuits would be provided.

Sandwiches of potted game and pounded chicken are given at

Afternoon Dances. Six dishes of sandwiches would be sufficient to provide, the cost of which would average from 9s. to 10s. if home-made potted-game were used.

Ham sandwiches average about the same.

Sandwiches are either cut into two-inch squares or into fingers of about an inch and a half wide.

Jellies, creams, and pastry are seldom given at Afternoon Dances.

In providing cups and saucers for an Afternoon Dance of a hundred guests, six dozen would be sufficient to have in readiness; the cost of hire of these is from 9d. to 1s. 6d. per dozen. Tea spoons, 6 dozen, hire 1s. 6d. per dozen.

Four dozen tumblers and three dozen wine-glasses would be required, the hire of which is 1s. per dozen.

When ices are given, 6 dozen ice-plates, and 6 dozen ice-spoons, would be necessary, the cost of the hire of which is from 1s. to 1s. 6d. per dozen.

When strawberries and cream are given, 6 dozen dessert-plates and 6 dozen forks and spoons would be necessary, the hire of which ranges from 1s. 6d. to 2s. per dozen. Coffee urns and tea urns are required for serving tea and coffee at an Afternoon Dance; the cost of hire of these urns, either bronze or plated, is from 3s. to 5s. per urn.

For cloak-room arrangements, see Chapter V, "Balls and Dances."

III

FIVE O'CLOCK TEAS AND "AT HOMES"

Five o'Clock Teas and "At Homes"—Large Teas—Small Teas—Professional musical arrangements for Large Teas—Fees to Professionals—Arrangements of Programmes—Mutual Accommodation System—Amateur Performers—Necessary arrangements of Reception Rooms—Serving Refreshments—Refreshments required—Cost of Hire of all requisite Articles—General Cost of the Whole.

Five o'clock teas and afternoon "At Homes" are not an expensive form of entertainment, even when given on a large scale, in so far as the refreshments are concerned; but if professional talent of a high order is engaged for the entertainment of the company, as is sometimes the case, this expense is entirely apart from the general expenses of ordinary teas, where amateur talent is considered sufficiently attractive for the occasion. In town, during the season when large and fashionable afternoon "At Homes" are given, it is usual to engage one or two celebrities in the musical world, whose talents lie either in the comic or operatic direction. The fees for such services range from 5 to 25 guineas; comic talent, however, whether English or foreign, is most in request at these reunions.

When invitations are issued for large "At Homes", at which a celebrity is to attend for the purpose of amusing the company, his or her name is written at the top of the invitation-card, that the guests may know the class of amusement provided for them; but when amateur talent is depended upon at these entertainments, the names of the amateurs are not written on the invitation-card, and the word Music is then written at the bottom of the card.

High-class talent, or *artistes* who are favourites and much in request in the fashionable world, naturally command a high price;

and ladies, whose only object is the success of their "At Homes" independent of cost, are glad to engage the most prominent talent of the hour, and consider themselves fortunate if another leader of fashion has not already appropriated the services of some talented lady or gentleman for the afternoon on which they themselves are desirous of engaging them. On the other hand, ladies to whom the expenses of an entertainment are a matter of some moment, and who can only afford a small fee, content themselves with engaging talent of a different order, the fees for these services range from 2 to 5 guineas, including pianists and vocalists.

There is also a very large class of afternoon teas, in which the musical part of the entertainment is arranged on a different system, which may fairly be termed the non-paying mutual accommodation system, and which works well as a rule, and answers the object in view, both parties deriving an equal amount of satisfaction from the arrangement.

Professors of music and singing—men of undoubted ability, but who, like many others, have their way to make in the world and do not find it ready made for them—are sometimes glad to give their services gratis at the houses of ladies possessing a large and fashionable circle of acquaintances, on the consideration of being presented to the most influential ladies present or those ladies who are likely to require professional services at their own parties, or professional instruction for their daughters. Such an arrangement as this, gives the *artiste* an opportunity of exhibiting his or her talents which might otherwise not be afforded; while the guests have the enjoyment of professional talent, and the hostess the *éclat* that professional talent always confers upon an entertainment.

This bringing forward unknown talent is not confined to ladies who work upon the mutual benefit system, as it may be termed, but is often followed by ladies wealthy enough to secure recognized talent for their entertainments, and who, from motives of kindly interest, lend a helping hand to rising talent by offering a suitable opportunity for its display.

Ladies inexperienced in the received mode of making a non-paying arrangement with professors, with whom they have a slight acquaintance, feel a delicacy in touching upon the question, and instead of speaking frankly, and coming to a direct understanding as to the terms upon which they solicit these professional services, they invite a musician to an afternoon tea in the hope that he or she will be good enough to entertain the company by the exercise of his or her musical abilities in return for the invitation card sent. This delicacy on the part of a hostess often places her and the musician in somewhat of a dilemma, she is rather nervous in the first instance as to whether he will sing or play at all when asked to do so, or whether, if he does comply with the request made to him, such compliance may not result in a charge being made for each song sung, while the musician naturally resents this underhand manner of obtaining his services. On the other hand, there are professors of all classes, whose merits range from superiority to mediocrity, and who on these occasions are beyond the pecuniary or self-interest question, and who when invited to afternoon "At Homes" exert themselves to contribute to the general amusement of the company, with the alacrity of an accomplished amateur. As an exception to this rule, there are professors who when invited to an "At Home" in the light of a guest, make a point of refraining from any exhibition of their respective talents, and who if pressed to sing or play make a charge the following morning for services rendered, but these extreme measures are seldom resorted to, and then only in the case of the hostess being all but a stranger to the *artiste*, and strongly suspected by him or her of having an *arrière-pensée* when issuing the invitation.

The number of performers engaged for an afternoon "At Home" varies from two to six and upwards according to the inclination of the hostess, and the programme of the music to be performed is submitted for her approval. Some ladies make a great point of supervising the programme, others leave it entirely in the hands of the *artistes* engaged.

A really taking programme, and one that most interests the guests at an afternoon tea includes the newest things of the hour, whether from operetta or opera-bouffe, or whether it be a chansonnette or pathetic ballad, novelty being the key-note of the selection.

The music of Offenbach, Lecocq, Halévy, Bizet, and Sullivan, &c., is apparently most appreciated at afternoon teas. Well-known operatic airs, gems in themselves, have been too often heard in the opera-house and concert-hall, not to lose by comparison when heard in a drawing-room where they only provoke disparaging comments on the powers of the *artistes* by whom they are rendered. Reminiscences of stars in the operatic world are so intimately entwined with the best known operatic airs, that a feeling of disappointment rather than pleasure is experienced by the listeners, who receive with satisfaction less ambitious and less well-known *morceaux.* A thing of beauty is a joy for ever, but at the same time it is irritating to hear a grand beautiful air indifferently sung, and when the vocalist, whether professional or amateur, does not possess talent of a high-class, it is unwise to attempt such a high flight; but singers, like other mortals, have a weakness to soar higher than their wings will carry them, and pass by the humbler yet surer goal that is within their reach.

Professional talent generally requires the use of a grand piano, while amateur talent is not so exigent, and is content with the one found in the drawing-room, whether it be an old grand or a new cottage. The hire of a grand piano ranges from 2 to 3 guineas.

Cane chairs and rout seats are seldom hired on these occasions, and the settees, sofas, and chairs, &c., of a drawing-room are usually sufficient to accommodate any average number of guests, and are ranged around the rooms, an ottoman being placed in the centre, space permitting.

Refreshments are served in the dining-room on a table arranged as a buffet at one end of the room; for further particulars on this head see "The Management of Servants." The usual refreshments given consist of tea, coffee, claret-cup, sherry, ices, cake, biscuits, and thin bread-and-butter.

In providing for twenty guests the allowance should exceed one-fourth of the quantities here given for eighty guests, but for every additional twenty guests *under* one-fourth would be the requisite quantities.

The quantities given in this and in every chapter are not arrived at from theory, but are the result of experience and observation, and may be confidently relied upon in every respect as being neither overmuch or over-little, but sufficient for all purposes. To some these weights and measures may perhaps appear trivial, viz., to those whose wealth enables them to despise small economies, but to the majority they will be of real value, as good housekeepers are well aware that the practice of small economies in housekeeping, not in one direction alone, but in every direction, is the secret of good management, enabling a moderate income to do its duty bravely and well.

Unnecessary expenditure and waste should not be attendant upon such social, frequent, yet unceremonious gatherings as afternoon teas, but from want of knowledge of the subject, the outlay for these modest entertainments amounts to twice the sum that need be expended, and mistakes occur of this nature, such as purchasing 6 lbs. of butter where 2 lbs. would be amply sufficient, or four quarts of cream where two would suffice.

Afternoon teas are dear to the hearts of all ladies, but especially so to those whose incomes do not justify them in offering a more expensive form of hospitality to their many friends, and with whom dinners and dances are hospitalities not to be thought of, and although a little dinner of six, it may be argued, is not such an expensive affair after all, yet it must be remembered that a dinner for six is not a banquet for sixty, that a dinner party is the reverse of elastic, while an afternoon tea possesses the elasticity of an India-rubber ball.

For instance, in providing for eighty guests, the quantities would average as follows:—4 gallons of coffee, allowing 6 ozs. of coffee to the gallon, thus, 24 ozs., or 1½ lb. of coffee, at 1s. 10d. or 2s. per lb., would amount to 2s. 9d. or 3s. according to the coffee selected.

If a smaller quantity of coffee were made, say for twenty-five guests, 8 ozs. should be allowed to the gallon. It is a very common mistake with givers of afternoon teas and "At Homes" to provide a far larger quantity of tea and coffee than can possibly be consumed; others, again, make a mistake in the opposite direction in providing too small a quantity, and thus the guests are kept waiting while a fresh supply is being made. The above quantity of coffee, viz., 4 gallons to 80 people, or 1 gallon to 20 people, will be found a correct allowance for afternoon at homes. The coffee is made in a receiver or copper, from which the urn or urns are filled. It is a great point, and one which is hardly enough studied, that the coffee given at these "At Homes" and afternoon teas should be very good; there is a tendency amongst those who dispense it, to be careless in this respect, and consequently the cups of coffee that are handed to the guests are hardly as palatable as a hostess would desire. When coffee is particularly good more is consumed than would otherwise be the case, but the proportion of 4 gallons to 80 people would be sufficient to meet all demands for coffee likely to be made at an afternoon "At Home".

The quantity of hot milk required is 1 quart to a gallon of coffee; thus a gallon of milk would be sufficient for 4 gallons of coffee; the cost of which would, at 5d. per quart, amount to 1s. 8d.

Care should also be taken that the milk served with the coffee should be at boiling point, and not merely lukewarm or tepid, as is too often the case.

For eighty people 4 gallons of tea would be required, or perhaps a little less, say 3½ gallons. A ¼ lb. of tea at 3s. per lb. is the proportion to each gallon; thus the cost of the tea required would be 3s., if 4 gallons of tea were made, or 2s. 3d. if 3½ gallons were made. When the water is hard an extra ounce of tea or coffee should be added to the gallon, while some cooks prefer adding a minute quantity of carbonate of soda. Tea, unlike coffee, does not improve by standing too long after it has been made, and it is, therefore, best to make it by the gallon as it is required.

An afternoon party lasts at least three hours, and a guest should be served with as good a cup of tea or coffee on departure as on arrival. Tea that has been made for three hours acquires that peculiar stewy flavour; the especial property of tea served to travellers at most railway station "Refreshment departments." An inferior tea, that is a cheap tea, should not be infused so long as a fine tea. A fine, thin leaf tea, whether green or black, should be infused from 10 to 15 minutes, and a cheap tea from 5 to 10 minutes.

The kind of water used has a great influence upon tea making. Soft water is the best; by soft water is not meant the presence of an alkali, but the absence or diminution in quantity of salts of lime, the hardening property in water. Distilled water, on the other hand, should not be used for tea on account of its being deprived of both air and minerals. Spring water is the best to use for making tea. River water ranks next, and well water last. The addition of soda to the water spoils the tea and renders it bitter, black, and unpalatable, yet it is sometimes necessary in very hard water which retards the extraction of tannin and colouring matter. The water should not be kept standing, but the trim or kettle should be refilled for every fresh infusion. It is the custom in Russia to use lemon-juice in tea in place of cream and sugar. This is supposed to improve the flavour of the tea; it does not injure it, and opposed as sugar and vegetable acids are to each other, the effect is the same, they are both ultimately changed into carbonic acid. The practice of drinking tea at five o'clock is injurious in a measure to those who have not eaten a good luncheon at between one and two; as to drink tea after several hours' fast produces irritability of the stomach.

Thus tea is beneficial after dinner or after a meal, on account of its powers of assimilation with regard to all kinds of food, and is injurious before a meal, producing general waste to the system, and not supplying nutriment, and it is allowed that tea does not promote digestion, although it increases assimilation. Tea is looked upon by many as a respiratory excitant; it induces activity of thought and wakefulness, but the reaction is in proportion to the quantity of tea drunk.

As boiling milk is essential to coffee, so likewise is good cream essential to tea. One quart of cream would be sufficient for 4 gallons of tea.

In town the price of cream is 4s. per quart, and in the

country 3s. per quart. 1½ pint of cold milk at 5d. per quart, is also requisite in case any of the guests prefer it to cream with tea.

4 lbs. of sugar would be actually consumed with the above quantities of tea and coffee; but it would be necessary to provide 6 lbs., for the purpose of keeping the sugar-basins well replenished. Thus 2 lbs. of crystallised sugar at 5d. per lb. would probably be used, and 2 lbs. of loaf sugar at 6d. per lb.

Tea and coffee are the chief refreshment given and most in request at afternoon "At Homes." It is, therefore, poor economy to attempt a saving in this direction by not providing what may be really considered "excellent," and the entire expense of tea and coffee, including milk, cream, and sugar, amounts to a very small outlay, even when first quality is provided. But little wine is drunk at afternoon teas, as the majority of the guests are ladies, and they seldom drink wine at this hour of the day. Sherry and claret-cup are the wines provided. It would be necessary, as a matter of convenience, to have four decanters of sherry on the table, each containing 1½ pint; although on an average 3 bottles of sherry would be all that would be drunk by eighty guests, supposing sixty of them to be ladies, although the amount of wine drunk at afternoon teas depends upon the number of gentlemen present, and it may be calculated that 1 bottle of sherry should be allowed for every ten gentlemen, taking into consideration the fact that if some men drink two glasses of sherry, others drink tea, coffee, or claret-cup in preference. Sherry at from 36s. to 48s. per dozen is considered a fair price to give for this purpose; but it greatly depends where the wine is purchased, and it may be either very good or very indifferent at the price mentioned.

Though claret-cup is invariably given at afternoon teas, it is less popular on these occasions than at lawn tennis and garden parties. It is drunk at garden parties because it is cool and refreshing, and people are more or less thirsty; but in town they seem to be rather afraid of it; and to have an impression that it does not suit them, and that it is, besides, rather too sharp or rather too sweet to please their palates, and it not unfrequently *is* one or other of these.

Half a gallon of claret-cup is considered a sufficient proportion for eighty guests at an afternoon tea, though not for a garden party, and the quantity required for half a gallon of cup is 2 bottles of claret to 2 bottles of soda-water.

Claret at 18s. per dozen is reckoned good enough for cup, but this again depends upon where the wine is purchased.

When ices are given at large five o'clock teas, during the summer months, the quantity required for eighty guests would average 5½ quarts. It would be necessary to provide 3 quarts for a party of 25, but 1 pint would be sufficient to add to this quantity for every additional ten guests.

The quantity would include two descriptions: ice, say raspberry and lemon, or pineapple and cherry. For the cost of ices, see page 36.

Wafers are given with ices; for eighty people 5 dozen would be sufficient, the cost of which would be 3d. per dozen if made at home, and 6d. per dozen if bought. The quantity of cakes, biscuits, and thin bread and butter consumed at afternoon teas is very small, but at the same time it is necessary that the table should be well supplied with these to avoid any suspicion of parsimony being attributed to the hostess.

Ornamental French confectionery is a feature on the buffet; it is pretty to look at, and gives the table a smart appearance, but, if much admired, it is but little eaten, and therefore is seldom provided, and most hostesses restrict their supply of confectionery to those things which from experience they are aware are generally preferred.

Almond macaroons are much liked by ladies, as are ratafias, cocoa-nut biscuits, chocolate-glacé biscuits, coffee biscuits, sponge biscuits; the cost of these are on the average 1s. 8d. to 2s. per lb.; sponge biscuits cost considerably less, being 6d. per dozen; sponge cakes, 1s. per dozen; 6 to 8 lbs. of these fancy biscuits would be sufficient. Pound cake is also liked, and 2 pound cakes, ranging from 2s. 6d. to 3s. each, would suffice, in addition to other things. Cake should always be cut into small, short pieces, easy to hold in the fingers, as large slices of cake are awkward to hold, as well as too much to eat with a cup of tea.

To provide sufficient thin bread and butter for eighty guests two quartern tin loaves, at 9d. per loaf, and 2 lbs. of fresh butter at 2s. per lb., would be required, and would make 4 or 6 fair-sized plates of bread and butter.

Many people, with whom economy is an object, do not indulge in fancy biscuits or rich cakes which run into shillings, if not into pounds, knowing also that a morsel of plain cake, or a slice of thin bread and butter, most commends itself to the generality of guests when drinking a cup of tea or coffee at an afternoon tea, and that when pretty and rich dainties are given they are a superfluity and an additional expense, and by no means a necessity. Thus, for a tea, or an "At Home" for eighty guests, the following quantities would be found sufficient: 4 Madeira cakes, at 10½d. each; 6 currant cakes, at 1s. each; 50 sponge cakes, at ½d. each; total for cakes and biscuits, 11s. 7d.; for bread and butter, the cost would be 5s. 6d., allowing 2 quartern loaves at 9d. a loaf, and 2 lbs. of butter, at 2s. per lb. With regard to tea and coffee, the quality and quantities before mentioned would be requisite, as it would be impolitic to make use of inferior qualities, and impracticable to reduce the given quantities.

Small households are necessarily not *monté* for the exigencies of an afternoon tea, but the hire of china and plate is so moderate that it is wiser to make a good provision in this direction than to rely too much upon the slender resources of the house; the attempt to make two or three dozen cups and saucers do duty for more than twice that number usually results in delay and confusion.

For an afternoon tea of eighty guests 5 dozen tea and coffee cups would be required.

The china-cupboard of the house would doubtless furnish 2½ dozen cups and saucers, in which ease 2½ dozen would be the number to hire, the cost being 1s. 6d. per dozen, and these should be, as soon as used, washed and replaced on the buffet ready for use.

The hire of 2½ dozen teaspoons would amount to 4s. 6d. at 1s. 6d. per dozen, half dozens being charged for as dozens. It is usual to hire both a tea and a coffee urn if the party is a large one, the cost of the hire of these urns is 5s. each, but when the party is a small one, this expense is unnecessary, and tea and coffee are dispensed from the usual sized tea and coffee-pots.

The cost of the hire of either tea-pot or coffee-pot is 2s., and of plated cream jugs or sugar basins is 1s. each article, but most houses are independent of this latter expense. When the tea is poured out from tea-pots, an urn with hot water is placed on the table. The china cupboard of a house is usually equal to supplying the number of plates required for the eatables; small plates are not used by guests at afternoon teas.

When ices are given ice-plates are of course required; the hire of glass ice-plates is 1s. 6d. per dozen. Three dozen of these would be sufficient. China ice-plates are a trifle cheaper, and cost for hire 1s. per dozen. If extra glass were required to that supplied by the house, the cost of hiring would be 1s. per doz. Any article that is damaged by chip or crack is charged for at its full value.

Every detail of the expenses connected with an afternoon tea have been here accurately stated; it would therefore be superfluous to give a total of the cost of an "At Home" or afternoon tea; this would be arrived at by a hostess herself, according to the quantities and costs here given, and also according to the style of refreshments selected by her and the resources of the house.

IV

GARDEN PARTIES

The Expenses attendant upon giving Garden Parties—Large Garden Parties given to the County—Small Garden Parties—Suburban Garden Parties—Garden Parties in Town—Arrangements suitable to each description of Garden Party—The various modes of serving Refreshments—The order of Refreshments given—The quantities required for a given number of Guests—Engaging a Band—Expense of a Band—Hire of Marquee or Tent—Amusements provided.

A GARDEN PARTY IS A popular and not expensive form of entertainment, as hospitality can be shown to a large circle of guests at a very modest cost. These afternoon garden parties take place from four to seven, but are only held as a matter of course from June to October. Garden parties are fashionable entertainments, and are frequently given on a very large scale. Royalty itself leads the way by giving afternoon parties to which from 800 to 1000 guests are invited, which is more or less followed by all ranks of society, including bishops in their palaces, officers in barracks, and members of yachting clubs on the lawns of the club houses, while in the suburbs of London these entertainments are very general, and in the country itself garden parties are an institution in every county, and the young ladies are able to count their invitations to them by the score. The ladies of each county consider it incumbent upon them to entertain their neighbours at least once or twice during the summer months, and those who have extensive grounds find that a garden party, of all entertainments, entails the least trouble and expense.

At large garden parties, where the guests assemble by hundreds instead of by tens, there is generally one or two military bands in attendance; if given by a regiment, assaults of arms take place at intervals for the amusement of the company.

Refreshments at these entertainments are invariably served indoors; but in the country refreshments at smaller garden parties are sometimes served in a tent, or on tables placed under the trees. At large garden parties tents of various sizes are erected on the lawn, and fitted up with seats in addition to the numerous chairs and garden seats that are indispensable, these are placed in rows in the vicinity of the band, and in all available shady spots.

At suburban or country garden parties rugs and Persian carpets are spread on the lawn under the trees, upon which seats are placed, so that should the grass be damp the guests need not fear taking cold.

The guests usually arrive from half-past four to five, and are received by their entertainers either on the lawn itself or in a tent, the names of the guests being announced by the butler or by the head-waiter.

Guests on their arrival usually inform their servants at what hour they purpose taking their departure, and expect their footmen to be in readiness at the time named to call up their carriages.

The usual run of garden parties given on a small scale averages from forty to one hundred guests, and in giving the details of the expenses consequent upon providing for a garden party, it is purposed to take the medium number, seventy-five; that in calculating the expenses for a larger or smaller number of guests it may be arrived at by adding to or deducting from this given number.

Lawn-tennis is now generally played at garden parties, so much so that garden parties are often designated lawn-tennis parties. In town and in the suburbs a military band is generally engaged to play from four to seven; in town a military band means the bands of the 1st or 2nd Life Guards, or that of the Royal Horse Guards Blue, and the bands of the Grenadier, Coldstream, or Scots Guards. These fine bands are a great attraction at a garden party, and a band belonging to either of these regiments can be obtained at the following barracks: Hyde Park, Regent's Park, Wellington, and

Chelsea Barracks, and at the Tower. The permission of the colonel of the regiment, or that of the "president of the band," has to be solicited as a matter of courtesy or form, when the bandmaster is applied to for his band, subject to this permission being granted. The cost of the band is regulated by the strength of its numbers, the charge ranging from 10s. to 15s. per man.

People who reside within twelve miles or so of London when they require a band to play at a garden party, usually apply to the nearest regiment quartered in their vicinity, such as Hampton Court or Hounslow, while those who reside in the neighbourhood of garrison towns, such as Woolwich, Chatham, Portsmouth, Dover, etc., have quite a choice of bands, and the cost of these averages 8s. to 10s. per man, and five guineas is the usual price to pay for twelve performers.

Those who reside at a considerable distance from a town where a regiment is quartered fall back upon the band of the county militia, yeomanry cavalry, or local volunteers; the cost of which bands average also from 8s. to 10s. per man, exclusive of railway fares and refreshments.

The usual refreshments provided for a band at a garden party consist of cold meat, ale, or sherry, or claret, as the bandmaster may prefer:—the cost of which would amount from 25s. to 30s.

Unless a garden party is given on the most economical scale, and it is desirable to spend next to nothing upon it, it is always advisable to engage a band, as the expense is small in comparison with the pleasure derived from it; but when a garden party is merely a small friendly gathering of from five-and-twenty to forty guests, the expense of a band is considered unnecessary, and its presence rather pretentious than not.

In providing garden seats and chairs for the accommodation of guests at a garden party, seats for one-third the number of those invited would be sufficient, in addition to the seats in the drawing-rooms, tea-room, and elsewhere.

Various descriptions of tents are usually erected at garden parties, umbrella tents, round wall tents, canopy tents, and small marquees.

The cost of hire of these tents and marquees ranges from £1 10s. to £20, according to size and description of tent.

Bright-looking Persian rugs for spreading on lawns can be bought from 9s. 6d. to 70s. each; the cheaper ones, although of coarser and commoner materials, answer the purpose equally well; although our trans-Atlantic neighbours, with their usual disregard of expense, make a grand display of handsome Persian rugs at their fashionable garden parties; but this comfortable custom may be followed without going to any considerable expense in the matter of rugs, always bearing in mind that old and faded hearth-rugs and mats have not an inviting appearance, and that squares of carpet do not offer sufficient resistance unless of the thickest texture—velvet-pile, Turkey, or Axminster. The ubiquitous crimson drugget, although available at all other entertainments, putting as it does a bright face upon much that is dingy in the way of carpets in corridors, landings, cloak-rooms, etc., is at a discount at a garden party.

The refreshments are almost invariably served in the house itself for several reasons—it entails far less trouble to serve refreshments in a tea-room, where all conveniences are at hand, than to arrange a buffet on the lawn under the trees. When it is desirable, however, that refreshments should not be served in the house from want of space, or some equally good reason, a large tent or marquee is hired for the purpose, the cost of the hire of which, say one 20 feet square, ranges from £3 and upwards; but, unless the guests number over one hundred, the expense of a tent for refreshments is seldom incurred, besides which a marquee is by no means a cool retreat on a sultry August afternoon, and a dining-room of a house, well ventilated and kept cool by the exclusion of hot air, is a far pleasanter resort for a large party of guests. Again, guests at a garden party find the change from the gardens to the house rather an agreeable one, and for this reason the reception rooms of a house or mansion are thrown open at a garden party, including drawing-rooms, library, billiard-room, or picture gallery if the house boasts of one.

The largest ground-floor room of a house, with the exception of drawing-room, is usually converted into a tea-room, in which tea is served on dining tables in the centre of the room, or from a buffet at the upper end of the room, as at an afternoon dance or five o'clock tea. Trays with refreshments are carried on to the lawn by the men-servants in attendance during the afternoon, and handed to the guests,—one servant carrying a tray with cups of tea and coffee, another a tray with glasses of sherry or ices.

The refreshments indispensable at a garden party are tea and coffee, sherry and claret cup, cake, and biscuits. Fruit and ices are given in addition to these refreshments when a saving of expense is not of paramount importance to the giver of an entertainment.

For a party of seventy-five guests, 1 lb. of tea would be used, 1½ lbs. of coffee. For price of tea and coffee, see Afternoon Dances. This quantity of tea and coffee would make 3 gallons of each, allowing a little over 5 ozs. of tea to the gallon, and 8 ozs. of coffee to the gallon. Tea should be made as required, in an urn holding 1 gallon, while the whole quantity of coffee is made in a 3 gallon coffee-kettle or copper; half this quantity should be served hot, and half as iced coffee in glass jugs, prepared with the proper quantity of milk and sugar, the coffee having been placed in ice some hours before required for serving. For further details, see Afternoon Dances, page 35.

Iced claret cup is also made as required, and 2 gallons is usually found sufficient for this number of guests, allowing 8 bottles of claret and 8 bottles of soda-water for the quantity of cup, in addition to about 2 lbs. of loaf sugar; the cost of this claret, at 18s. the dozen, would amount to 12s.; the price of soda-water, as has been before said, ranges from 1½d. to 3d. per bottle, according to where it is purchased.

Badminton averages the same as does claret cup. Champagne cup and Moselle cup are but seldom given, but when provided, sweet champagne or sparkling Moselle, the former at 42s. and the latter at 36s. per dozen, would be good enough for this purpose. The same quantity of either of these wines would be required for this as for claret cup, viz. 8 bottles of wine to 8 bottles of soda-water, but the quantity of cup drunk at a garden party depends upon the number of gentlemen present, and also whether they are players of lawn-tennis, in which case there would probably be a run upon iced cups; thus less than 2 gallons, or more than two gallons, would be drunk, according to circumstances. When matches of lawn-tennis are played at a garden party, a table is placed on the lawn, with iced drinks, sherry and seltzer-water, for the benefit of the gentlemen. Sherry and seltzer is rather a favourite drink with men in general, and 6 to 8 bottles of sherry would probably be drunk, or even less, according to the number of gentlemen present; thus, from 1 to 3 dozen seltzer-water would be required, but, as has been before said, it entirely depends upon how many gentlemen are present.

In some remote counties, for instance, the gentlemen at a garden party are represented by three or four young curates and two or three old gentlemen, while the ladies perhaps muster from forty to fifty, in which case very little wine is drunk. When garden parties are held in or near London, or in the home counties, or in or near cathedral cities, in or near university towns, and garrison towns, &c., the numbers are more equal, and generally one-third of the guests are gentlemen; therefore, a hostess, when providing wine for a garden party, naturally takes this into consideration.

When ices are given, 5½ quarts would be a good proportion for seventy-five guests. The cost of water-ice, if made at home, is from 1s. 6d. to 2s. per quart, according to the flavouring selected; if bought at a pastry-cook's, the cost is from 5s. to 7s. per quart.

With regard to fruit, the cost in town entirely depends upon the day's market price; it is always cheaper in the country than in town, and if not to be had from the gardens of the givers of an entertainment, it can always be obtained at a very reasonable price from a market gardener in the neighbourhood. Strawberries and cream are a popular dainty, but somewhat an expensive one to give, and in providing it a sufficient quantity would be required for two-thirds of the guests present.

Strawberries, when sold in large quantities, are usually sold by the pound, and not by the punnet or basket; thus for seventy-five people from 8 lbs. to 10 lbs. would be a fair proportion, averaging from 1s. 6d. to 4s. per lb., and the supply of cream necessary to the above quantity of strawberries would be from 3 pints to 2 quarts, allowing 1 quart of cream to 5 lbs. of strawberries. Early strawberries are not served with cream but rather as dessert, and two to four dishes would probably only be provided when the price runs high. These are placed on the tables and not served from the side table, as are strawberries and cream when served in any quantity. All other fruit is provided in the same proportion as dessert is provided, that is to say, two to four dishes of each kind, according as the hot-house and gardens yield, or according to the expense to be incurred in the purchase of fruit.

For cost of cakes and biscuits see Afternoon Dances, and for the requisite quantities for seventy-five guests, deduct one-fourth from the quantity there given for one hundred guests.

For cost of hire of all necessary glass and china for garden-parties, and for the number of articles required for use, see Chapter II, Afternoon Dances, and deduct accordingly from the quantities there given, or add thereto in proportion to the number of guests invited.

Refreshments are served from 4 to 7—from the commencement to the termination of a garden-party. Two women-servants should pour out the tea and coffee; a third should serve either ices, or strawberries and cream, when given, while the guests help themselves to all other refreshments on the tables, whether to fruit, wine, or cup, etc. One man-servant should also be in attendance in the tea-room, to offer any assistance in the way of opening soda-water or pouring out wine. An attendant is hardly required in the cloak-room, unless the party is a very large one, as ladies are not always shown into the cloak-room on their arrival at a garden-party, and many ladies prefer to leave their wraps and dust cloaks in their carriages.

In some counties Archery Meetings are a great feature in the amusements of the summer months, and the expenses of these are sometimes defrayed by the club itself; but archery-parties are very often given to the members of the county archery club by the gentry of the county. These parties are given on various scales of hospitality, from a mere afternoon-party to a dinner, dance, and supper. In the former case refreshments are served in the house or in a tent or marquee, erected in the vicinity of the targets. In the latter light refreshments are served from 4 to 7; a cold collation is served in a large marquee at from 7 to 7.30; dancing takes place at 9 in either dining-room or drawing-room; for cost of hire of band for dancing, see Chapter on Afternoon Dances. Tea and coffee, etc., are served until 12, when a supper, on the principle of a ball supper, is given. The cold collation or dinner is more substantial than a ball supper, as cold lamb and cold beef are given, and bowls of salad, in addition to ham, tongues, chickens, mayonnaises, and various sweets, jellies, creams, pastry; for cost of which see Chapter on Balls and Dances, as well as for cost of archery supper.

With regard to the quantity of roast beef and cold lamb required for a party of one hundred, in addition to the other viands, 16 lbs. of beef and 16 lbs. of lamb, say leg, loin, and shoulder, would be an average proportion; the cost of both averaging 1s. per lb.

Sherry and claret are given at this description of cold dinner, and the proportion of claret drunk on these occasions is twice that of sherry. Thus for a party of one hundred, 3 dozen of claret would be an average quantity, and 1½ dozen of sherry; for cost of which see Dinners, Chapter XI. For cost of hire of marquees and large and small tents, see Chapter V, Balls and Dances. For the quantities of plate, glass, and china required, and for the cost of hire of the same, also for cost of hire of chairs, tabling, etc., see same chapter

For the description of refreshments given during the evening, see p. 70. Ices are not always given at these gatherings, and when given generally consist of two descriptions of water-ice. With respect to the style of supper given on those occasions it is usually of the simplest order of ball-supper; neither hot nor cold expensive *entrées* nor expensive sweets being provided, as the guests principally comprise very young people of both sexes, and upon whom a supper of expensive dainties would be more or less thrown away; for *menus* of suitable suppers, see Chapter V.

In providing wine for an archery dance supper, considerably less would be required than for an ordinary ball supper, given in either town or country. Thus for a party of one hundred people, supposing seventy of the number were ladies, 3 dozen champagne would be sufficient, in addition to 1 dozen of sherry; for cost of wine, see p. 27, Chapter I.

V

BALLS AND DANCES

The Expenses attendant upon giving Balls and Dances—Large Balls—Dances—Small Dances—Large Balls given on a grand scale of Expense—Dances more popular and numerous than Large Balls—General Ball-room arrangements—Preparing Floors—Ventilation of Rooms absolutely necessary—The best method of ventilating Ball-rooms—The use and misuse of Bunting—The charge for covering in Balconies—The hire of Awnings—Floral decorations—Lighting—Musical arrangements for Balls and Dances—Military Bands—Number of Performers necessary—Charge for the same—Quadrille Bands—Piano Bands—Tea-room Refreshments—Method of Serving—Order of Refreshments provided—Quantities required—Supper-rooms and Supper-tables—Temporary Supper-rooms—Large and small Supper-rooms—Waiting at Ball-Suppers—The number of Waiters required—The class of Waiters to be avoided—The class of Waiters to be engaged—Where and how to obtain good Waiters—Waiters' charges—The arrangements of the Supper-tables—The hire of Plate, Glass, and China—Requisite quantities—Lighting—Various styles of Suppers—Fashionable dishes—Soups —Hot entrées—Hot roasts—Grosses pièces—Entrées froides—Entremets—Quantities and cost of the same—Wines given at Ball-Suppers—The probable quantity drunk by a given number of Guests—Menus for Ball-Suppers

BALLS ARE A VERY EXPENSIVE form of entertainment, and one from which the most hospitably inclined not unnaturally shrink. Those whose ambition it is to give a good ball and to do things well, as it is termed, not unfrequently spend from three to five hundred pounds upon one ball, and oftener than not the verdict of their friends and acquaintances is "everything was very well done, but it was a great crush." These large expensive balls, costing from £300 to £500, and at which from 300 to 500 guests are present, are now seldom given by the *élite* of society. Here and there, however, those accustomed to give their annual ball during the London season, still continue to do so, while with the *nouveaux riches* this lavish style of entertaining commends itself in preference to a less pretentious one. It offers scope for spending money and for carrying out the arrangements for a ball in a manner which shall indicate in ever so slight a degree the possession of great wealth, wealth upon which they take their stand in society, and therefore they gladly take advantage of this outlet for its display.

What is now termed a "dance" has in society almost superseded and put out of countenance its elder brother, the old "ball." At these fashionable "dances" the number of the guests ranges from 80 to 200, which latter is the outside number of a really enjoyable dance, but when the number is extended to 250 to 300, as it not unfrequently is by inexperienced and easy-going dance-givers, the element of enjoyment is eliminated, the space at command not being elastic in proportion to the demands thus made upon it.

To give a thoroughly pleasant and successful dance there are many points to be considered which are too often overlooked by those with whom expense is no object. The givers of large balls and crushes are under the impression that if their rooms are not crowded almost to suffocation with panting, perspiring humanity, it will not be considered a sufficiently full ball, therefore when not possessing a "dear five hundred friends," invitations are accorded to their friends' friends' friends, people the ball givers have never seen before, and who most probably they would not care to see again. The reverse of this idea is the pivot upon which experienced hostesses work when making arrangements for giving a dance; they limit their invitation list to a given number of guests, and having determined this number in accordance with the size of their rooms or the space at their disposal, they cannot be persuaded to exceed it. Not only do they allow for proper ventilation and free circulation through their rooms, but they also allow for the possibility of dancing, the *raison d'être* of the gathering, just the one point in the entertainment which so many givers of dances and balls are in the habit of overlooking. They provide with no lack of expense or trouble music, flowers, lights, and supper, and the numerous etceteras which go to swell the cost of a ball or dance, but the one thing that would make the ball or dance a success and a pleasure, is omitted, viz., sufficient space to gyrate in the round dances, which are the dances of the period. A quadrille might, perhaps, be danced upon a hearthrug, but Lancers, again, require a given space, without which they are divested of elegance and grace, and the movements of the dancers are in consequence cramped and stiff, if not absolutely awkward.

There are other *désagréments* in a crowded ball-room besides want of space for dancing and the inconvenience entailed upon the non-dancers, foremost of which is the over-heated and close atmosphere of the rooms, and the consequent inhaling of vitiated air by those present, the result of over-crowded rooms and the partial if not total exclusion of fresh air by means of closed windows on the one hand, and covered in balconies on the other. There is no doubt that the lassitude and fatigue often experienced by ball-goers is attributable to breathing this pernicious atmosphere, rather than to the healthful exercise of dancing, or to the attendant late hours. This is equally true of the largest ball or of the smallest carpet dance. Wherever an extra pressure is put upon space by the congregating together of a number of individuals immensely over and above the legitimate number that the rooms should contain, these results must ensue; therefore, as the necessary breathing space cannot perforce be given, it is imperative for the comfort and health of the guests that the atmosphere of the rooms should be constantly renewed by the admission of fresh air.

The ventilation of a ball-room by means of open windows offers the objection of causing a draught, more particularly felt by those persons occupying seats beneath and near the windows, and this is no doubt the reason why the windows of a ball-room are so persistently closed, besides which, the draught from a half-open window causes the wax lights to flicker and gutter in a most unpleasant manner, to the detriment of gentlemen's coats and ladies' gowns. The absurd practice of covering in a small narrow balcony and surrounding the windows of a ball-room, to the total exclusion of air, has already been commented upon in a former work,[1] and we are glad to be able to record that a slight improvement has taken place in this direction, and that two small apertures or openings are occasionally introduced into these closed balcony awnings, which openings are draped with lace curtains, but these small apertures, about the size of a lattice window, are still quite inadequate to the occasion. The ventilation of a ball-room is a matter of such importance, that instead of being completely overlooked it should be one of the first, if not the first, point for consideration.

One simple and successful mode of ventilation is to remove the windows from their frames and to replace them with draperies of muslin or lace, and to place large blocks of ice on the balconies that the fresh air may be still further cooled before passing into the ball-room itself.

The registers of the stoves should remain open, so as to carry off heated air. The non-observance of this rule causes the air of a ball-room to become hot and oppressive in a very short time.

In giving a ball or dance the supper is looked upon as the one paramount expense to which all other expenses are subordinate. Indeed, these minor expenses are so little considered after the one great expense has been effaced, that ball givers are sometimes not a little surprised, at the sum total these expenses represent when the various bills are sent in.

To commence with one of these minor expenses, but an all-important one in its way, the floor of a ball-room. The drawing-rooms or drawing-room of a house is, in town, the room usually converted into a ball-room, save in those stately mansions which boast of an especial ball-room or picture-gallery of noble proportions, wherein these festive entertainments are held; in these handsome apartments the flooring is kept in a highly-polished condition, and only requires a little extra polishing on the occasion of a ball being given. The flooring of many a London drawing-room now also presents a polished surface, parquet flooring being so much in vogue; but an ordinary flooring, even in those houses that are of recent build, requires to be thoroughly put in order by the aid of a carpenter, all the unevennesses of the surface to be planed, and the boards prepared for polishing. The cost of this is simply the workman's time, which may be either three days or three hours according to the size of the rooms and the condition of the boards.

Although there are several preparations recommended for preparing floors for dancing, there is none that is so thoroughly satisfactory as is the wax polishing process. When a preparation of turpentine is used, the strong odour it emits clings to the room for days, which no amount of fresh air or essences can influence for the time being.

A sticky preparation, formed of bees-wax and other ingredients, is sometimes used with even worse results; the floor attains a gluey and an adhering surface, in lieu of a smooth and polished one, particularly destructive to the trains of dresses and to satin boots and shoes. The floor of a ball-room should present the appearance of a mirror, and be entirely free from every loose particle of wax, and to produce this effect is simply a matter of labour: the rubbing bees-wax into the boards by means of brushes loaded with lead. The cost of such labour is according to the state of the boards and the size of the rooms, and may be estimated at 6d. per square yard.

A floor that has once been polished in this manner should not subsequently be scoured by an energetic housemaid, as it could be put in excellent dancing order by a small amount of labour, and thus made to realise a valser's beau-ideal of what a floor should be.

For small and unpretentious dances—the little dances that young ladies persuade their mothers to give, while confidently assuring them that they will cost hardly anything—this mode of preparing the floor is not entertained on the ground of expense, and all the preliminary arrangements are of the simplest possible character; for instance, after the aid of an inexpensive carpenter has been secured—one working on his own account and not sent out by a large firm—the floor having thus been put in order, is rubbed with powdered French chalk until it presents a decidedly slippery surface. This rubbing can be easily done by the domestics of the house assisted by the children, who greatly enjoy the amusement of sliding up and down the rooms. Dancing on a polished floor, however, whether it be a fashionable dance or the most modest little piano dance, means the displacing of all the moveable furniture of a drawing-room and taking up carpets, and consequent inconvenience to the family in general. Thus when the number of invited guests is under one hundred, a dancing-cloth is placed over the carpet; this is more especially done when dances are given in the winter months, when the inconvenience caused by taking up carpets is more felt than in the summer.

Those who frequently give carpet-dances, as they are called, generally buy a dancing-cloth in place of hiring one. The cost of purchasing a dancing-cloth would be according to the size required, and averages 1s. per square yard; these cloths last a considerable time with careful usage and occasional cleaning and reglazing. The cost of hire of a dancing-cloth ranges from 10s. to £2 2s, or 6d. to 9d. the square yard. Putting down these cloths is a separate expense, and is charged either by the hour or by the job, and no injury is done to a carpet when these cloths are properly put down, as they are fastened with large brass studs.

With regard to the number of seats placed in a ball-room, if the room is a very spacious one, it is usual to place settees or rout-seats around the walls and in the recesses of the windows and in other available spots.

When the accommodation of a house admits of it it is usual to fit up one smaller room as a drawing-room; but when dancing takes place in both drawing-rooms, and there is no third room at command, then an extra number of rout-seats are provided in the ball-room, on the landings, and in the tea-room. The hire of rout-seats with velvet cushions is from 4d. to 6d. per foot, or with damask cushions at from 3d. to 4d. per foot. In allowing for seating of guests at a ball or dance, seats for one-third of the number invited would be sufficient, as two-thirds of the company at a ball or dance are either dancing or going to and fro to the tea or supper room, and therefore not more than one-third of the guests are seated in a ball-room at one and the same time. Thus, for a party of 150, 50 feet of seating would be sufficient, in which would be included the settees and small chairs furnished by the house; the cost of covering in balconies and of awnings averages 1s. 6d. per foot, and covered corridors connecting a ball-room with a supper-marquee is at the same rate.

When more accommodation is required for a supper-room than the dining-room of a house affords, a marquee or temporary room is erected, notably in the summer months; the cost of a temporary room varies according to the internal arrangements, ranging from 6s. to 9s. per foot—the expense of linings for the roof and the walls and the solidity of the floor causing the difference in the price.

A less substantial structure than a temporary room, viz., a marquee or tent, can be had at 2s. 4d. per foot if unlined and undecorated, and at 7s. 6d. per foot if lined and decorated, and the floor covered with carpet or cloth.

A temporary room or marquee 30 feet by 20 feet would be large enough to accommodate a party of 150 guests at a sit-down supper, allowing half the number of guests to be seated at table at one time.

The prevailing idea with most people is that a ball-room cannot be too brilliantly lighted; those who can afford it indulge in a positive blaze of light, and in addition to the usual centre chandelier or gaselier of a drawing-room, half circles, containing from nine to twelve wax lights, are suspended from the walls at the most convenient points, interspersed with girandoles with from three to twelve lights.

Others again consider that this blaze of light should be judiciously toned down, being softer to the eyes and more becoming to the ladies. Thus the wax lights are shaded with coloured shades, and the globes of the chandeliers and gaseliers with tinted glass or coloured muslin, while the more economical ball-givers reduce the number of lights and limit themselves to what is absolutely necessary to render the ball-room a fairly well if not a brilliantly lighted one;

thus the cost of lighting a ball-room or, more properly speaking, in many cases a drawing-room prepared for a dance, depends upon the number of lights hired, as well as the number of candles used; the hire of half-circles and girandoles for walls is 1s. per light, and chandeliers average the same price, 1s. per light; the cost of wax candles, at four to the pound, to burn six hours, are from 1s. 4d. to 1s. 6d. per lb.

Balconies, conservatories, and out of door corridors and gardens, are often lighted with Chinese lanterns and coloured lamps; the former are usually placed in conservatories and corridors, and the latter amongst shrubs and trees.

The lanterns are bought at from 3s. to 30s. per dozen, and the coloured lamps are hired at from 30s. to 42s. the 100, trimmed and ready for use.

Hanging lamps and lamps on brackets for lighting halls, staircases, and passages, can be hired at from 2s. to 3s. each.

The extent of the floral decorations of a ball-room, staircase, or entrance-hall, is entirely a matter of inclination; the cost of which may range from £1 to £100. Wealthy ball-givers, and ball-givers possessing country estates, adorn their rooms with the choicest roses and exotics, convert their entrance-halls and corridors into leafy bowers by the aid of stately palms, evergreens, and foliage plants. In most cases the cut flowers are sent from the home conservatories in the country, and the flowering plants and shrubs hired by the dozen, or the whole supplied by contract.

People who cannot afford to do things well in this department often prefer dispensing with floral decorations altogether to making a meagre display; while others take a medium course, and at a small expense, yet with an extra amount of trouble, make as good a show as possible upon the sum expended, confining their outlay to clustering evergreens and foliage plants and a few fragrant cut-flowers, ignoring the use of flowering plants in pots altogether, as so many of these would be required to make a suitable display.

In small rooms as well as in large ones, it is always advisable to remove the door of the front drawing-room, and to drape the doorway with *portière* curtains, which have a prettier effect than an open door, and cause no inconvenience to the dancers; the door of the back drawing-room should also be removed and draped with curtains or altogether closed.

The seats for the band or the orchestra, as they are termed, are placed at the upper end of the front drawing-room—space permitting—or, failing this, in the back drawing-room. The strength of the band depends upon the size of the rooms, or the expense to which the host is inclined to go.

If a string band, the number of performers ranges from nine to twenty-four, and the charge is from 17s. to £1 per man, whether the band were the string baud of a regiment or a quadrille band.

In the country, or in the neighbourhood of garrison towns, a military band or a militia band of from nine to twelve performers can be engaged to play at a ball or dance at from five to six guineas. The above charges do not include in either case railway or other expenses.

A piano band is usually engaged for a small carpet-dance, and consists of two performers only—a pianoforte player and a cornet player; the charge varies from £1 10s. to 3 guineas, according to the standing of the musicians. For after-dinner dances, when only one performer is engaged, viz., a pianoforte player, the charge is £1 1s.

A convenient cloak-room is required for the use of the ladies, and a ground-floor room is most suitable for this purpose, however small it may be. A general cloak-room of which both ladies and gentlemen have admission does not offer sufficient privacy and comfort for the ladies as does a small room set apart exclusively for their use, where torn dresses can be re-arranged, and curls and caps readjusted, and little accessories to the toilets for these purposes should always be provided. Thoughtless hostesses are apt to overlook such trifles as these, and to consider that if the duplicate number of a cloak ticket is given to a lady, nothing further is required in the cloak-room for her convenience.

Cloak labels can be bought by the dozen, and the most convenient way is to roll up the cloaks and wraps belonging to each party and place them in rows on a table with a number attached to each cloak or roll of wraps, the corresponding number being given to the owner.

One or two women servants should be in attendance in the ladies' cloak-room according to the number of guests invited.

A cloak-room is also always provided for the gentlemen, with toilette mirror, &c. The overcoats are taken by the man-servant in attendance, rolled separately and placed on tables, and numbers attached to each as with ladies' cloaks. When space is limited, and the cloak-room is not larger than a mere cupboard, coat-racks are used instead of tables. Gibus hats are always taken by the gentlemen into the ball-room, and are not given up with the coats; while hats that are not Gibus are placed with the coats.

The groom of the chambers, or a servant out of livery, conducts the guests on their arrival into the cloak-room.

The library, smaller dining-room, or breakfast-room, or other ground-floor sitting-room of a house, is arranged as a tea-room; the front dining-room being required for a supper-room is not available for this purpose, unless supper is to be served in some larger room, such as a billiard-room, or in a marquee or temporary room erected for the occasion.

If the tea-room is a small one, seats are not placed around it, but if it is a commodious apartment, seats are placed in convenient recesses and corners. Tea and light refreshments are served from a buffet placed at one end or at one side of the room, and occupies the whole length of it. The buffet or tea-table is covered with a white table-cloth; the urns containing tea and coffee are placed in the centre of the table; the cups and saucers are placed within easy reach of the servants engaged in pouring out the tea and coffee, while the jugs containing hot milk and cream, together with basins of sugar, are placed the length of the table within reach of the guests.

The light refreshments provided in the tea-room consist of Tea, Coffee, Claret-cup, and Sherry, and various descriptions of cakes and biscuits, all of which are placed on the table. Ices are not placed upon the table, but are handed by the servants in attendance when asked for. (See "The Management of Servants.")

For a party of 150, 7½ gallons of tea would be required, and 7½ gallons of coffee, allowing 4 ounces of tea to the gallon, at 3s. per lb., and 8 oz. of coffee to the gallon, at 2s. per lb.

In arranging for a party of guests under 150, the requisite allowance of coffee would be at the rate of 1 gallon to 20 people, and of ten the same quantity.

Fifteen pints of hot milk would be required to 7½ gallons of coffee; 4 pints of cream would be required to 7½ gallons of tea. When cream is not given, and economical people sometimes curtail this expense, 7 pints of cold milk would be required to this quantity of tea. On the other hand when cream is given, it is a great improvement to the tea, and is rather expected by tea-drinkers, while to hosts hospitably inclined, the saving of 6s. 7d. in this direction is not a matter of great importance, although when the line is closely drawn, the old adage holds good, "Take care of the pence and the pounds will take care of themselves." Six pounds of sugar would be provided, and about 4 lbs. actually consumed.

Iced claret-cup is always given, and, if good, is much drunk by the guests; eight quarts would be sufficient to provide for a party of 150.

To make this quantity of cup eight bottles of claret and eight bottles of soda-water, in addition to sugar and ice, would be necessary: half this quantity should be made in readiness, and the remainder supplied as wanted.

Claret suitable for cup can be bought at 18s. per doz. The average cost of soda-water is 1s. 6d. per doz.; thus the cost of 8 quarts of cup with all ingredients would amount to 14s. 6d.

Besides claret-cup, sherry is the only wine drunk in the tea-room. 1 dozen of sherry would be the average amount drunk by the guests present; young ladies, as a rule, do not drink sherry before supper. Decanters of sherry are placed the length of the buffet or tea-table that the guests may help themselves.

Sherry at 48s. per dozen is an average price to give, but the quality of the wine greatly depends upon where it is purchased. Pale sherry is, as a rule, more liked than brown sherry, but it is always advisable to provide both brown and pale sherry.

Seltzer water and soda water are often asked for by the gentlemen present; thus, 3 dozen of each would be required, the cost, of which is 1s. 6d. per dozen. A liqueur case containing two bottles of brandy would be placed on the sideboard in the event of its being required; brandy at 6s. to 7s. per bottle is a usual quality to give.

Orangeade, lemonade, cherry water, negus, &c., are not given at fashionable balls and dances, but at juvenile parties only.

Ices are invariably given at a dance or ball; for a party of 150, 10 quarts would be an average proportion. Two kinds of water ice are usually given, say strawberry and pineapple or lemon and raspberry. If made at home the cost of these ices would be 1s. 6d. per quart, using fresh fruit in the summer, and preserved fruit in the winter. If bought at a confectioner's, the price varies from 5s. to 8s. per quart according to the ice chosen, from lemon to peach, and also according to the standing of the confectioner. When supplied by the dozen the charge is from 8s. 6d. to 12s. per dozen.

Thus sufficient water ice for 150 people, if made at home, would cost 15s., while an equal quantity, if purchased, say at the rate of 6s. per quart, would cost £3.

Cream ices are sometimes given, in which case half the quantity required for a given number of guests would be cream ice, and half the quantity water ice. Cream ice can be made at home in town at 4s. per quart, and in the country at 3s. per quart. When bought at a confectioner's the price is from 6s. to 9s. per quart, under the same conditions as before mentioned, the ice selected, and the standing of the confectioner. Five dozen ice wafers would be required to this quantity of ice; if made at home the cost of these would average 3d. per dozen, and if purchased, 6d. per dozen.

With regard to cake, biscuits, &c., the following quantities would be the proportion for 150 guests. Four pound cakes, 2s. 6d. each if made at home; 12 lbs. of macaroons, ratafias, and fancy biscuits, at

1s. 6d. per lb.; 2 lbs. of coffee biscuits, 1s. per lb. and 6 dozen sponge biscuits at 6d. per dozen.

Whenever a saving of expense in this department is required, rice cakes at 1s. each, and Madeira cakes at 10d. each, can be substituted for pound cake and for the more expensive description of fancy biscuits.

For a party of 150, 8 dozen cups and saucers is a convenient number to have in readiness, although 6 dozen could be made to suffice if a sufficient number of servants were in attendance. The cost of hire of cups and saucers is from 9d. to 1s. 6d. per dozen according to where they are hired. Teaspoons, 1s. 6d. per dozen. Plated tea and coffee urns are usually charged 5s. each. Four dozen ice plates would be required for a party of 150. The rate of hire for ice plates is from 1s. to 1s. 6d. per dozen, and of ice spoons 1s. 6d. per dozen. Five dozen wine glasses would be required for use in the tea-room, in addition to 3 dozen tumblers and 1½ dozen soda water glasses. The rate of hire of these glasses is from 9d. to 1s. per dozen.

Refreshments are served in the tea-room until the hour of supper.

There are various styles of ball-suppers given, suppers on a grand scale, suppers on a medium scale, suppers on a small scale, heavy suppers and light suppers, smart-looking suppers and homely substantial suppers, and last, but not least, suppers made by the home *chef* or home cook, and suppers "sent in" from a confectioner; but in many cases three times the quantity is provided beyond what is actually required, the reason of this being no doubt the difficulty in arriving at the average quantities required for a given number of guests, rather than the desire that the hospitable board should be overladen with delicacies. Much unnecessary expense would be avoided if ball suppers were served *à la Russe* and the tables adorned only with flowers and fruit, but this mode of serving supper would entail too long an absence from the ball-room on the part of the guests, besides requiring an extra staff of attendants; and even as supper is now served, notably sitting-down suppers, a good staff of servants, is required, far larger than is needful at standing-up suppers, but when practicable, the former mode of serving supper is followed. When economy, however, is at the helm of affairs, or even when want of space renders it expedient, standing-up suppers are given.

Whether the supper be a sitting-down or a standing-up one—whether it be an expensive or an inexpensive one—the one thing to aim at is to have everything of the best of its kind, either fish, flesh, fowl, or fruit, and to achieve this result the home department is the one to rely upon.

Supper is invariably served in a ground-floor room, either in dining-room, library, or billiard-room, whichever offers the greatest amount of accommodation for the purpose, or failing these it is served in a marquee erected for the occasion, the price of which is regulated by the size required, and the number of guests to be accommodated; at the cost of so much per foot, see p.67.

A greater amount of tabling is required for a sit-down supper than for a stand-up supper. For the former, 18 inches are usually allowed to each cover, for the latter 12 inches are considered sufficient.

The arrangement of the supper-tables depends upon the size of the supper-room. From four to ten small round tables are usually provided, in addition to one long supper-table, or two long tables, according to the number of guests to be accommodated; and as few supper-rooms in town are capable of accommodating more than eighty guests at one time, it is usual to provide sitting or standing room for half the number of guests invited; thus the company find their way into the supper-room in two detachments (See "Manners and Tone of Good Society.")

When it is not possible to provide sitting accommodation for more than one-fourth of the guests invited, seats are placed at round tables only, and not at the long tables. Therefore, those who prefer being seated at supper, take their turn at the round tables as the places are vacated. When a stand-up supper is intended, no compromise is attempted in the way of introducing seats or small tables into the supper-room, and the orthodox 12 inches space is frequently reduced to 9 inches, if not less.

The usual cover for supper, whether sit-down or stand-up, consists of a large knife and fork and a glass for champagne; similar covers are given at both long and round tables. The supper itself is arranged on the long table—the dishes being placed with a due regard to the convenience of the guests on either side of it.

The soup is handed by the servants in attendance, as is also the hot *entrée* when one is given.

Although it is customary for guests to help themselves to the cold things on the supper-table, yet when there is a good staff of servants in attendance, ready to offer any assistance required in the matter of helping from a dish, or bringing help from dishes at the further end of the table, the supper is served in a more expeditious and satisfactory manner.

In engaging waiters to assist at a ball-supper, care should be taken to select experienced, active men, thoroughly acquainted with the method of waiting at table; and equal care should be taken to avoid obtaining the services of fat, heavy, sleepy-looking men, a type of individual usually "sent in" by the purveyor supplying the supper. Waiters such as these are slow, awkward, and inattentive; if not deaf they are at least dull of comprehension, and require an order to be twice or thrice repeated before they appear to understand it. They have also an objectionable habit of wheezing and puffing and breathing hard when pouring out wine, and wait altogether in a slovenly untidy manner, and will, if not sharply looked after, mistake a glass that has been used for a clean one, when pouring out wine for a fresh arrival at the supper-table.

Every ball-goer is more or less acquainted with these fat, unwieldy waiters, and are aware of the class of service to be expected from them.

Smart-looking waiters, thoroughly up to their duties, are the class of men that should be engaged to wait; they serve the supper in a superior manner as regards the arrangement and the replenishment of the dishes, and otherwise contribute to the comfort and convenience of the guests. Good waiters are not obtained without a certain amount of trouble; but as the same price is paid per night to either class of waiter, it is expedient to secure the best service.

Honesty and sobriety are also important points in the character of a waiter, as a certain amount of risk is incurred when admitting a staff of strange servants into a house on an occasion when so much valuable portable property in the way of plate is temptingly at hand.

At grand entertainments given by foreign official personages, it is not unusual to have a detective on duty for the purpose of guarding the plate; less exalted personages, however, are content with making strict inquiries into the characters of the waiters they engage. Usually a trustworthy butler possesses a certain number of acquaintances whom he is able from personal knowledge to recommend as good and efficient waiters; but in the case of a butler not feeling confident of being able to secure the assistance of waiters for whose honesty and general capabilities he is in a position to vouch, the steward of any good club of which the master of the house is a member, or the manager of an hotel, are the best authorities to refer to, and through whom good waiters may be easily obtained.

When waiters are hired through the confectioner by whom the supper or part of the supper is supplied, he is supposed to be responsible for their honesty and sobriety; but as the appearance and manner of the waiters to be engaged is of importance to ball-givers, they should insist upon the waiters being seen and questioned by the butler, or failing him should take the trouble of doing so themselves. By this means the services of the picked men for an establishment are secured, over the ruck of indifferent waiters whose merits mainly consist in being just able to wear a limp white tie and a seedy-looking black coat. The practice adopted by second-class waiters of making a general raid upon the supper-tables, even before the whole of the guests have dispersed, is very much deprecated, and conscientious servants will not permit this to be done; others, regardless of the interest of their masters, allow unopened bottles of wine and untouched dishes to be enjoyed and carried off by the waiters, not unfrequently taking their own share of the spoil, in the shape of some half dozen bottles of wine, &c. To guard against practices such as these, and to avoid the unseemly and disagreeable spectacle presented by waiters, who, if not exactly tipsy, have yet drunk enough wine to become both stupid and boozy, it should be thoroughly understood that beyond a substantial supper of cold beef, bread and cheese, and beer, provided for the waiters, the ball-supper is to be respected by them, save what the butler may think proper to add to the cold meat-supper after the ball is over, in the way of fragments from the various dishes. Unless these precautions are taken and a certain amount of firmness is exercised by those in authority, the wine bill for eighty guests will probably amount to a sum which would suffice for wine for double that number. This is no exaggerated view of the unnecessary expense and waste that result from careless management. As an instance in point it was found that in comparing two separate accounts of wine supplied, the one for ninety guests, the other for one hundred and eighty, the quantity purported to be consumed was identical, and although a large margin must in every case be allowed for the difference that always exists between the quantity of wine consumed by a given number of guests against a similar number, yet the discrepancy here mentioned was far too wide of the mark to be accounted for under this head. In engaging waiters to wait at a ball-supper, the usual proportion is one waiter to every fifteen guests; thus for one hundred and fifty guests ten waiters would be required, or eight waiters might suffice, if a saving in this direction were considered necessary.

At a stand-up supper probably half this number of waiters would be engaged, more particularly if the supper-room were a small one.

When waiters are engaged to wait, two of the number arrive in the afternoon, to assist in arranging the tables, these receive one guinea each; a third waiter acts as announcer, his charge is also one guinea. The waiters who arrange the tables in the afternoon wait in the tea-room during the evening; the remainder of the waiters engaged arrive shortly before supper, and receive from 12s. to 15s. per man.

The butler has charge of the wine and superintends the arrangements in both tea and supper-room; the footmen in livery are stationed in the entrance-hall, and do not wait in the supper-room. The extent of a ball-supper is regulated by the pocket and inclination of the giver of a ball or dance. Thus in discussing the momentous question of the expense of a supper, with regard to quantities and qualities, each class of supper must be taken into consideration, from the ultra-fashionable to the most unpretending. At an ultra-fashionable supper, in addition to every description of cold delicacy that the mind of a *chef* can conceive, a hot *entrée*, a hot roast, and one and even two soups are given. Many again give one hot *entrée* and one soup to supplement the cold dishes; but the general run of ball-givers do not provide either hot *entrées* or hot roasts, although soup is considered indispensable at all fashionable suppers. For a party of one hundred and fifty guests 20 quarts of soup would be required.

Allowing 20 lbs. of shin of beef at 7d. per lb., and 10 lbs. of knuckle of veal at 8d. per lb., with the necessary vegetables, this quantity of clear soup, viz. 5 gallons, can be made at home at the cost of £1 0s. 4d., while if purchased at a confectioner's it would amount to £4, the lowest price of clear soup being 4s. per quart. If the ball is a late one an extra supply of soup would be required to serve to the few remaining guests on their departure; for this purpose 1 gallon would be allowed in addition to the 20 quarts or 5 gallons already mentioned.

Thick brown soups, such as mock turtle, mulligatawny, oxtail, are never given at ball suppers; white soups are occasionally given, but only in addition to clear soup. When a white soup is given it is either *Crême de Volaille, Soupe à la Reine,* or *Soupe à la Palestine;* the cost of these if made at home would average 2s. per quart, and if supplied by a confectioner from 5s. to 6s. per quart.

When two soups are given the proportion is usually 14 quarts of clear to 6 quarts of white.

Consommé d'Esclignac is much given at fashionable suppers, the cost being similar to the white soups before mentioned 2s. per quart when made at home.

The usual mode of serving soup at ball suppers is in soup cups.

The hot *entrée* given at a ball supper consists almost invariably of cutlets, either of lamb or mutton, according to the season of the year, *Côtelettes d'Agneau aux Petits Pois, Côtelettes d'Agneau à la Macédoine,* being preferred. For a party of 150, 8 dishes of cutlets would be the proportion, allowing 12 cutlets to each dish, which would be served in relays throughout the supper; the cost of this *entrée* would amount to £1 9s., allowing 24 lbs. of lamb at 1s. per lb., the average being 4 cutlets to the pound, and 5s. for vegetables for *Macédoine,* &c.

A hot *entrée,* although always given at a ball-supper or large dance supper, is seldom given at small dance suppers.

In the country the hot *entrée* consists of game, either partridges or pheasants *Gibier découpé,* but as this *entrée* is made from game reared in the home preserves, it would be difficult to arrive at the exact cost.

Hot roast chickens are sometimes given in addition to cutlets by very wealthy ball-givers; for a party of 150, 8 chickens would be the proportion, the cost of which, at 7s. per couple, would amount to £1 8s. The only vegetables given with this hot roast are asparagus or green peas; the cost of these entirely depends upon the market price and the season of the year.

Amongst fashionable preludes to the general cold supper, oysters take high rank, *Huîtres au naturel,* but when given, they not unusually take the place of a hot *entrée* and hot roast, and are principally provided at small dance suppers during the winter and early spring months, where the guests average from 80 to 90; thus, for a party of 90, with a fair proportion of ladies, 40 of whom may be taken not to be oyster eaters, 20 dozen oysters would be a fair proportion to provide; the cost of oysters usually averages 3s. per dozen, thus 20 dozen would amount to £3.

The usual mode of serving oysters at a ball supper is to place ½ a dozen oysters on a supper plate to every alternate cover. Oysters are always greatly appreciated by men, if not by ladies; it is therefore advisable to go to a little extra expense on this head, and give something that is really liked by those who do not, as a rule, affect *entremets* and sweets.

Six plates of thin brown bread and butter would be required to this given quantity of oysters, in addition to 6 lemons cut into half quarters; the cost of this would amount to 5s. The lemon, pepper, and vinegar, are handed by the servants in attendance.

There are certain *grosses pièces* which repeat themselves at every description of ball supper; they include ham, tongue, chickens, turkey, game, and game pies, and appear respectively on the *menu* as, *Jambons de York à la Gelée, Langues de Boeuf-decorée, Poulets rôtis aux Cressons, Dinde farce aux truffes, Faisans rôtis, Pâté de Gibier.*

For a party of 150, 2 hams would be provided, one of which is usually cut into thin slices, placed on various dishes and garnished with aspic jelly; it then appears on the *menu* as *Jambon découpé à l'Aspic*; the cost of 2 hams weighing 16 lbs. each would amount to £1 12s.

Two tongues would be the proportion for the above number of guests; 1 of these would also be served *découpé* with aspic jelly. The cost of these tongues, if home cured, would amount to 10s., or if bought already cured to 15s.

Cold roast chicken is a safe supper dish to provide, it being particularly in request amongst ladies. It is not always at a ball-supper that a roast chicken is the tender morsel it should be, but when an experienced home cook has the inspection, as well as the roasting of the said chickens, her vigilant eye will not allow of an old hen finding its way to the supper table under pretence of being a fine young capon. The cost of chickens much depends upon whether they are bought in town or in the country, or whether they are home reared, while the number required for a party of 150 would be regulated upon the number of roast pheasants provided. If game were in season, and 4 roast pheasants were given, 6 chickens would be sufficient to provide; out of the game season, 10 chickens would be needed. The price of chickens in town varies from 6s. to

9s. per couple, while they may be ordered from a country farm at from 5s. 6d. to 6s. per couple.

"Chicken" appears in many forms upon the *menu*, even as a *grosse pièce*, without taking into account its presence amongst the *entrées*, where it plays a conspicuous part. As a *grosse pièce* it is respectively styled *Chapon à la Perigord*—meaning a capon dressed with truffles—*Poularde* and *Poulet*. The price of a capon varies from 8s. to 14s. according to size.

The difference between a *Poularde* and a *Poulet* is that the former is a fuller grown bird than is the latter. *Poulet rôti aux Cressons, Poulet à la Béchamel, Poularde à la Flamande*, &c., &c., as they appear on the *menu*, are roast chickens served with a different garniture or a different sauce.

Roast turkey is a general favourite *grosse pièce*. A turkey weighing 16 lbs. stuffed with truffles, tongue, and forcemeat, would be an average size to give. Putting the turkey at 1s. per lb, the tongue at 4s. 6d., the truffles and other ingredients at 3s., the cost of the whole would amount to £1 3s. 6d.; this dish appears on the *menu* as *Dinde farce aux truffes*. Those who do not wish to go to the expense of using tongue and truffles in dressing a turkey, use forcemeat stuffing, and garnish the dish with aspic jelly.

During the game season it is usual to give cold roast pheasants at ball suppers, on which occasions they divide the honours of the table with the cold roast chickens, an equal number of each being given. Pheasants when purchased in the London market vary from 6s. to 9s. a brace, according to their size and the state of the market.

Game pie is a very popular dish at a ball supper, and is very generally liked; 2 large game pies would be the proportion for a party of 150, the cost of which would average one guinea each when made at home.

A boar's head, or *Tête de Sanglier farce aux truffes*, is a very imposing *grosse pièce* to give during the winter months; the cost of which, if prepared at home, would amount to 15s., and if purchased ready dressed, from 25s. to 2 guineas.

Galantines of game or chicken are occasionally given amongst the *grosses pièces*, but oftener amongst the cold *entrées*. When served as a *grosse pièce*, probably a galantine weighing from 8 to 10 lbs. would be provided; this could be made at home at 1s. per lb., or for even less in the country.

Spiced beef, glazed beef, braised beef, or roast beef, are not given at ball suppers, not being included amongst fashionable supper dishes. The cold *entrées* or *entrées-froides*, that form no small portion of a ball-supper, may be classed thus—the substantial and the moderate, the epicurean and the expensive.

Those who wish to make their ball supper a feature, as it were, go largely into smart and special cold *entrées*, while others limit themselves to providing what is conventional, *en règle*, necessary, and sufficient for the purpose, but with regard to the requisite quantities; those who are most desirous of keeping within bounds, often outstep them in the matter of expense through not knowing the correct proportions required when ordering dishes for a ball-supper.

When expensive *entrées* are given, it is found sufficient to provide for one-third of a party of 150 guests. For 200 or 250 guests the proportion of each dish would be for one-fourth. On the other hand, the cold *entrées*, or *entrées-froides* as they are termed, which are general favourites, and suit the palates of the many rather than of the few, are provided for in the proportion of one-half; or two-thirds when the party does exceed 150; over that number, with regard to many of the dishes, the proportion would decrease to one-third.

Pâté de Cailles is one of the before-mentioned expensive *entrées-froides*. The proportion for a party of one hundred and fifty would be 4 dozen *pâtés*; the cost of quails averages from 10s. to 15s. per dozen.

Chaudfroid de Cailles, Galantine de Cailles, Croustade de Cailles, belong to the class of *entrée*, and are provided in the same proportion as are *pâtés*, and the cost is similar.

Mauviettes à la Lucullus is another fashionable *entrée-froide*. These larks are stuffed with oysters or with truffles; one oyster or one truffle to each lark. The price of larks ranges from 2s. to 3s. per dozen; 4 dozen larks would be the proportion for a party of one hundred and fifty, to the expense of these must be added 4 dozen oysters at 2s. per dozen.

In selecting *entrées* of this description variety is studied as much as possible, thus larks and quails would not appear on the same *menu*.

Bouchées de Crevettes is an equally fashionable *entrée*; the cost of prawns for making this dish usually ranges from 1s. to 1s. 6d. per dozen; 4 dozen *bouchées* would be the proportion.

Pâté de Foie Gras is served in various ways, such as *Pains de Foie Gras, Foies Gras à la Régence, Timbales de Foie Gras*, &c. The cost of either of these would range from £1 10s. to £2 2s.

Galantine de Caneton is a favourite spring *entrée-froide*; the cost of which for one-third of a party of 150 would amount to £1 2s., putting the ducklings, of which this dish is composed, at 9s. per couple.

Various *entrées-froides* of pigeons are given during the spring months, such as *Chaudfroid de Pigeon, Chartreuse de Pigeon, Pigeons en Bellevue*; 2 dozen pigeons would be sufficient for an *entrée* of this description, and for the given number of guests above referred to; the cost of this, putting the pigeons at 1s. 6d. per couple, would amount to £1 3s., allowing for extra ingredients.

Two or three cold *entrées* of chicken are usually given at a ball-supper, and are selected from the following:—*Poulets en Assiettes, Mayonnaise de Volaille, Grenades de Poulets à la Doria, Salades de Poulets à la Russe, Chaudfroid de Poulet, Rémoulade de Poulet, Poulets decoupées à la Béchamel, Galantine de Poule, aux Truffes, Suprême en Surprise, Poulet à la Tartare, Chartreuse de Volaille*, &c.

When three descriptions of *entrée-froide* of chicken are given, it would be sufficient to allow 3 chickens to each *entrée*. If 2 chicken *entrées-froides* were given, 9 chickens would also be required.

In the spring, when chickens are very small and proportionately expensive, it is more economical to give *entrées-froides* of chicken than to give roast chickens, as chickens dressed with tongue, truffles, forcemeat, or salad make good *entrées*.

The usual price of chickens during nine months of the year is, in town, from 6s. to 8s. per couple, and in the country from 5s. 6d.

to 7s., according to weight. In the spring months they average, in town, 9s. per couple, and in the country 7s.

In estimating the cost of chicken *entrées* 3s. should be allowed to each *entrée* for salad, cream, truffles, tongue, &c., or whatever other ingredients may be required for any particular *entrée*. Chicken *entrées*, purchased at a confectioner's, average from 10s. 6d. to 12s. 6d. per dish; but even at this price one must not be surprised if sometimes they are found to consist of fillets of old hen rather than of young chicken; but *que voulez-vous?—il faut vivre.*

"Salmon" and "lobster" appear in almost as many different forms at a ball-supper as does chicken; the former as *Saumon à la Macduff, Escallopes de Saumon-Norvégienne, Mayonnaises de Saumon, Saumon à la Montpellier, Tranches de Saumon à la Tartare, Saumon à la Parisienne, &c.,* and the latter as *Buissons de Homards à la Tartare, Salades de Homard, Mayonnaise de Homard, Darioles de Homard, Aspic de Homard, Souffle de Homard Glacé.*

Both salmon and lobster are in such demand at these entertainments, that it is usual to provide in proportion for two-thirds of the guests as regards some of the dishes mentioned, and for one-half of the guests as regards others.

At some ball-suppers salmon is served *en pièce* of from 20 to 25 lbs., at others it is served in either of the ways before mentioned. For a party of 150, 26 lbs. of salmon would be provided if served whole, which at 3s. 6d. per lb., the average cost of salmon, would amount to £4 7s. 6d.; but if served as *Tranches de Saumon*, 20 lbs. would be sufficient, and 15 lbs. for either *mayonnaises* or *escallopes*, in which case 5s. must be added to the cost of the salmon for ingredients wherewith to dress it.

People who give economical ball-suppers do not attempt salmon, knowing that there is certain to be a run upon it if good, and it is a useless waste of money to provide other than the freshest salmon; salmon that has been over-iced, with a view to keeping it, has a whitish and pallid look about it, and is both rough and dry to the palate.

When lobsters are given, 6 lobsters would be the proportion, at from 3s. 6d. to 4s. 6d. each, for making salads, mayonnaises, and other *entrées-froides*, to which 10s. to 15s. must be added for necessary ingredients. *Salade de Homard* is very generally eaten at ball-suppers, and this manner of dressing a lobster is rather economical than not.

When lobster is served as mayonnaise, 8 lobsters would be used at the before-mentioned price, allowing 6s. for ingredients, cream, &c.

If served *en aspic* 8 lobsters would be required, and 6s. allowed for ingredients for aspic. The same number of lobsters would be required for the *entrées* before-mentioned, in addition to 6s. for ingredients.

Dressed crab is very little given, in fact it is not considered fashionable. Yet, when people depart from the strict line of fashion and give dressed crab, it is well received by the guests, in other words done justice to.

When served as *Pain d'Ecrevisses à la Gelée*, it is, on the contrary, considered a smart dish; but when crab is given in either of these forms, to provide for one-sixth of the guests present would be sufficient, allowing two fine crabs at 4s. 6d. each, and from 1s. 6d. to 2s. 6d. for the various ingredients required.

Filets de Soles, Mayonnaise de Soles, Sole en Aspic, are occasionally given by way of variety, and by way of economy; here again only one-sixth of the guests need be considered with regard to this fish *chaudfroid*, the cost of which would average 8s., allowing two pairs of soles at 3s. per pair, and 2s. for either aspic or cream, &c.

"Collared eel *en Aspic*" is another *chaudfroid* of fish, and only moderately popular, and in providing this dish the same rule holds good for the preceding one, namely, to allow for only one-sixth of the guests; from 7s. to 8s. would be the cost of the required quantity. Sandwiches of potted game, chicken, or lobster are invariably given; four good-sized dishes of sandwiches, sufficient for one-sixth of the guests, would cost from 6s. to 8s.

In providing *Entremets*, a great deal or very little may be spent; here, again, the ultra fashionable and the wealthy are prodigal in this direction, while less wealthy and economical ball-givers content themselves and endeavour to content their guests with a few modest jellies and creams interspersed with inexpensive *pâtisseries*; but every *menu* comprises jelly, and in providing jelly it is customary to allow sufficient for two-thirds of the guests present, jelly being very popular with ladies. Thus sixteen jellies of one-and-a-half pint each would be the quantity required. It is usual to give two or three kinds of jellies, as variety is gained at no additional expense. The most fashionable jellies are *Gelée à la Macédoine, Gelée au Marasquin, Gelée de Noyeau, Gelée Printanières au Champagne*. Calves'-foot jelly is not given at ball-suppers, and jelly is invariably made of isinglass, the cost of the quality used being 8s. per 1b. Gelatine at from 3s. to 3s. 6d. per lb. is occasionally substituted for jellies flavoured with liqueurs; but jellies made from gelatine are in every way inferior to those made from isinglass, and are neither so clear, bright, nor flexible.

Macédoine jellies are usually made in quart moulds, and liqueur jellies in pint-and-a-half moulds; the cost of the former averages, when home-made, 3s. 6d. per quart, and of the latter 2s. 6d. per mould; allowing 4 oz. of isinglass to the one, and 3 oz. to the other. When made of gelatine the cost is less by 1s. per quart.

The usual price of jellies when bought at a confectioner's is from 5s. to 8s. per mould, according to the jelly ordered, and to the size of the mould, *Macédoine* being the most expensive. The creams usually given at ball-suppers are *Crème de Fruit, Crème de Café, Crème de Fraises, Crème à l'Italienne, Crème au Marasquin, Crème de Framboises, Crème à l'Ananas;* of these one or two are selected for a ball-supper, and it would be sufficient to provide for one-third of the guests. Thus, for a party of 150, 8 creams would be sufficient, the cost of which would average 4s. per cream, flavoured with fresh fruit, while if flavoured with essences they would average 1s. less per mould; but home cooks are not allowed to substitute essences for fresh fruit. A confectioner's charge for fruit cream is from 6s. to 8s. per mould.

Home-made *Crème de Café* is far less expensive than is *Crème de Fruit*, and averages 2s. 4d. per mould.

Chartreuse de Fruit is a smart *entremet* to give, either *Chartreuses d'Abricots, Chartreuses de Framboises, Chartreuses de Fraises,* &c.

Macédoines de Fruits are also given, the proportion being for one-fourth of the guests; thus four quart moulds, or six pint-and-a-half moulds, at from 3s. to 4s. per mould, according to the season and to the fruits chosen, would be sufficient for the before-mentioned number.

It is usual to give one or two *Gâteaux*, either *Gâteau Napolitan, Gâteau Bordeaux, Gâteau Bretagne, Gâteau à la Suisse, Gâteau Génoise glacé*. The cost of either of these cakes, if made at home, would vary from 5s. 6d. to 7s. 6d. according to size, and from 7s. 6d. to 12s. 6d. if bought at a confectioner's.

Nougat à la Cambacères, Petits Savarins au Punch, and other descriptions of light French confectionery, are provided, although but very little in demand.

This light confectionery, which is supposed to put the finishing touch to a well-arranged supper-table, includes sweets of the following order:—*Puits d'Amour, Petits Savarins, Surprises au Chocolat, Bouchées à la Crême, Pain à la Duchesse, Pain de Mecque, Génoise glacé, Darioles à la Parisienne, Franchanettes à la Vanille, Nougat à la Crême, Éclairs au Café, Meringues glacées*, &c. &c. Any of these, if made at home, would cost on an average 1s. 6d. per dozen, but are rarely attempted by other than a French cook, as they can be purchased at a confectioner's at from 3s. to 4s. per dozen; and 4 dozen of these assorted sweets would be a fair proportion for the above number of guests.

The wine is always a great feature at a ball-supper, and by the class of wine given the supper itself is estimated. If the wine is good the supper is pronounced to have been a first-rate one, if the wine is bad the supper is said to have been a bad one; and it not seldom follows that where the wine is excellent the supper is good also; but there are houses where the supper is all that it should be and the wine very inferior, and sometimes the reverse is the case, and the finest brand of champagne is given, say at 120s. per dozen, with a supper that reflects anything but credit upon the cook or the confectioner. Every man fancies himself to be a judge of wine more or less, and many ladies imagine that their judgment may also be relied upon to distinguish good wine from bad; but nevertheless there are both men and women who are very dense in this respect, and cannot discriminate between gooseberry champagne and Irroy's 1864.

On the other hand there are men who are keenly alive to the quality of the wine offered them at ball or dinner; they do not expect that a host will offer the choicest vintages his cellar contains to be drunk at a ball or dance, but they have an unpleasantly long memory for any shortcomings in the champagne given them.

Many ball-givers make a point of giving the very best champagne to their guests, knowing that this part of the entertainment reflects directly upon a host rather than upon a hostess; that he is responsible for the wine provided. Thus, if his pocket will not allow of his giving very superior champagne, he exerts himself to procure the best he can at his price, that he may not blush for the brand, should a curious guest be tempted to examine a champagne cork with a view of ascertaining the brand he has been imbibing. There are men who are either curious or absent-minded enough to do this in the houses of those individuals with whose cellars they are not thoroughly acquainted.

Champagne is always given at a ball-supper, at a dance numbering 50 guests, or at a ball numbering from 200 to 300. The quantity of champagne drunk varies considerably, the hour at which a ball terminates governs it in a great measure, depending upon whether it terminates at 2 A.M. or continues until 4.30 A.M., or whether the majority of the men are under twenty or over thirty, whether they have dined quietly at home, and drunk 2 or 3 glasses of light claret, or whether they have come on from a dinner-party where each man has drunk from half to three-quarters of a bottle of champagne. Thus, in providing wine for a party of 150, 5 dozen champagne, 2 dozen sherry, 2 dozen claret, would be a very fair proportion. The price of champagne usually given at ball-suppers varies from 60s. per dozen to 96s. per dozen.

Seltzer-water and soda-water are very much in demand at ball-suppers, and 6 dozen of each would be the quantity to provide. The price of these aërated waters is 1s. 6d. per dozen. Some ball-givers provide a variety of mineral waters, apollinaris, &c., in addition to soda- and seltzer-waters, which are drunk with either champagne, sherry, or brandy. The liqueur-stand, containing 2 bottles of brandy, is placed on the sideboard: brandy at 7s. per bottle is the quality usually given.

The cost of hire of plate, china, and glass is as follows: silver-handled knives, 1s. 6d. per dozen, ivory-handled knives, 1s. per dozen; table-forks and spoons, 2s. per dozen; dessert-spoons, 1s. 6d. per dozen; plated dishes for serving hot *entrées*, from 1s. to 2s. per dish; soup-tureens, plated, from 4s. 6d. to 6s. each; china soup-tureens, 1s. 6d. each, but for a ball-supper plated tureens are preferable, as the soup does not so soon get cold as when served from a china tureen. The cost of hire of china dishes of all sizes is from 2s. to 4s. per dozen; soup plates and supper plates, 1s. per dozen; soup cups from 1s. 6d. to 2s. per dozen.

A centre-piece with lights can be hired at from 5s. to 7s. 6d., according to its style of ornamentation, while the hire of épergnes ranges from 3s. 6d. to 10s. each; assiettes montées, 3-tier, for fruit, from 3s. 6d. to 10s. each. The finest grapes or strawberries, &c., surmounted by a pine, are arranged on these stands; thus the fruit forms a conspicuous ornament on a supper-table.

The hire of champagne-glasses ranges from 1s. to 1s. 6d. per dozen, and the hire of wine-glasses and tumblers from 9d. to 1s. per dozen; the hire of decanters is 6s. per dozen or 6d. each.

A supper-table is usually lighted with candelabras, holding from 3 to 12 wax-lights; the cost of hire of these ranges from 3s. to 12s., according to the number of lights, averaging 1s. per light. The number of candelabras would be regulated according to the length of the table and the size of the room.

Whenever it has been practicable the cost of dishes ordered at a confectioner's has been given side by side with those made at home, to enable a ball-giver accurately to arrive at the expense from both points of view, that is, having a supper made at home or ordering the whole, or even a part of the whole, dish by dish.

When a ball-supper is contracted for at so much per head, it is entirely given into the hands of a confectioner, who engages to provide, in addition to the supper, all necessary plate, china, glass, seats, tabling, flowers, and light refreshments in the tea-room; the charge for this, not including wine, ranges from 8s. 6d. to one guinea per head, according to the style of supper required. At the lowest price neither soup, hot *entrée*, hot roast, nor smart dishes, are given, but only the most inexpensive meats and sweets; at the highest price, viz., a guinea per head, soup, a hot *entrée*, a hot roast, and a variety of delicacies in and out of season are given. Thus a plain supper for 150 guests at 8s. 6d. per head, would cost, irrespective of wine, £63 15s., and at half-a-guinea per head £78 15s.; at 15s. 6d. per head the cost for 150 guests would amount to £116 5s. 0d., and the *menu* provided at this price, although not over-luxurious, is yet sufficiently comprehensive. The cost of various styles of ball-suppers made at home, including light refreshments for the tea-room, from the plain to the luxurious supper, ranges from 3s. 6d. to 10s. 6d. per head.

MENU FOR NOVEMBER, DECEMBER AND JANUARY

MENU

Potage
Consommé d'Esclignac

Entrée Chaude
Gibier découpé

Grosses Pièces

Jambon à l'Aspic
Pâté de Gibier aux Truffes

Langue décorée
Dinde

Entrées Froides

Mauviettes
Mayonnaise de Volaille
Côtelettes à la Princesse
Timbales de Foies Gras
Jambon découpé à l'Aspic

Suprême en Surprise
Salades de Homard

Galantine de Gibier
Langue découpé à l'Aspic

Entremets

Macédoine de Fruits
Gelée de Noyeau
Crème à l'Italienne

Gelée au Marasquin

Bavarois au Café

Puits d'Amour
Chartreuse de Fruits

Gâteau Napolitain
Darioles à la Parisienne
Pâtisseries Assorties

MENU FOR MARCH AND APRIL

MENU

Potage
Consommé Jardinier   Crème de Volaille

Entrées Chaudes
Côtelettes d'Agneau à la Macédoine   Poulets Rôtis

Grosses Pièces
Galantine de Chapon aux Truffes
Jambons de York à la Gelée   Langues à l'Écarlate
Poulardes à la Béchamel

Entrées Froides
Chaudfroid de Cailles   Grenades de Poulets
Salades de Poulet à la Russe   Langues découpées en Bordure
Buissons de Homards à la Tartare
Pâté de Fois Gras à la Régence
Oeufs de Pluviers en Aspic   Sandwiches Régence
Escallopes de Saumon-Norvégienne
Mayonnaise de Filets de Soles

Entremets
Gelées Printanières au Champagne   Gelée au Marasquin
Crême à r'Ananas   Crême au Noyeau
Pains d'Abricots aux Liqueurs
Gâteau Bretagne   Petits Savarins au Punch
Bretons à la Moderne   Nougats à la Cambacères
Bavarois à la Reine

Pâtisseries

MENU FOR MAY AND JUNE

MENU

Potage
Consommé Clair

Entrée Chaude
Côtelettes d'Agneau aux Petits Pois

Grosses Pièces
Chapons à la Perigord   Poulets aux Cressons
Langues de Boeuf
Jambon de York   Pâté de Gibier

Entrées Froides
Pâté de Cailles   Pains de Foie Gras
Chaudfroid de Poulet
Galantine de Caneton   Bouchées de Crevettes
Tranches de Saumon à la Tartare
Mayonnaises de Homard   Remoulade de Poulet
Canapés à la Reine   Pigeons en Bellevue

Entremets
Gelée à la Macédoine   Gelée au Maraschino
Gelée à la Vin de Madère
Crême de Mille Fruits   Crême de Framboises
Chartreuse de Fraises
Babas aux Fruits   Gâteau Napolitain
Pâtisseries   Pain à la Duchesse

Eclairs au Chocolat

MENU FOR JULY AND AUGUST

MENU

Potage
Consommé Clair

Grosses Pièces

Jambon de York   Dinde Rôti
Langue de Boeuf Poulets Rôtis

Entrées Froides

Mayonnaise de Poulet Salade de Homard
Pâté de Gibier   Soles en Aspic

Entremets

Gelée de Maraschino   Gelée Vin de Madère
Crême au Café   Crême de Fraises
Bouchées à la Crême
Surprises au Chocolat   Gâteau Suisse
Pâtisseries

VI

RECEPTIONS, ASSEMBLIES AND "AT HOMES"

Various scales of Expenses incurred in giving Receptions, Assemblies, "At Homes," Official Receptions, Large "At Homes," Small "At Homes"— General arrangements—Tea-room and Supper-room arrangements—Light Refreshments—Quantities required—Various styles of Suppers

THE TERM "RECEPTION" IS PRINCIPALLY applied to evening parties given by persons occupying official posts and by persons of rank and position, at which the guests number from 200 to upwards of 800.

An "Assembly" is the old-fashioned appellation for what is now known as a "Reception;" it signifies the same style of entertainment, and is given by the same order of persons, viz., those belonging to the upper ranks of society.

An "At Home" is an elastic entertainment given by the members of different sections of society, and which may be given at a considerable expense or at a minimum of expense.

Receptions, as their name implies, are only held in large mansions, which can boast of a fine suite of rooms, where all arrangements are carried out on an extensive scale of hospitality.

Flowers, plants, palms, and exotics adorn the rooms and staircases. Cut flowers and exotics are usually provided from the home gardens and conservatories, while flowering plants, shrubs, ferns, palms, &c., are generally contracted for at a London nursery.

In mansions where the reception-rooms are replete with every description of art treasure, bronzes, statuary, china, paintings, tapestries, marbles, carvings, frescoes, &c., &c., floral decorations are in a great measure dispensed with, and are principally limited to cut flowers and foliage plants.

A reception usually lasts three hours, commencing at 10 P.M. Saturday receptions, however, terminate at 12.30, and on all other nights of the week at 1 and 2 A.M.

At official receptions, or receptions given on a large scale, a military band is engaged, and plays selections of music at short intervals the whole of the evening; it is stationed in the vestibule, corridor, or at the foot of the grand staircase. The cost of providing a band for this purpose is according to the strength of the band sent out, and ranges from 12s. to 15s. per man.

At other receptions, and "At Homes," the amusement is provided for the guests in the way of any novelties that may be the fashion of the hour, such as minstrels, bands of singers, and other foreign celebrities or comic talent, represented by either old or new favourites, or a drawing-room recital is given by some leading actor or actress of the day, for which latter performance a fancy price is often paid, in accordance with the ephemeral popularity of the performers, but as a rule the cost of providing this class of entertainment at "At Homes" varies from 5 to 50 guineas.

Some givers of receptions and "At Homes" consider it incumbent upon them thus to provide amusement of some especial character for their guests, while others think this unnecessary.

The *raison d'être* of many receptions is to meet a royal, foreign, or celebrated personage, while others are given merely as sociable reunions, and to which celebrated personages are not invited, and for which popular musicians are not engaged.

At all "At Homes," whether large or small, light refreshments are served for two hours, from ten until twelve, in the tea-room. These usually consist of tea, coffee, sherry, ices, cake, and biscuits, similar to the light refreshments described in Chapter V, "Balls and Dances."

In providing tea and coffee for a reception or "At Home," 6 gallons to every 100 guests would be an average proportion, 3 gallons of tea and 3 of coffee. With regard to the quantity of tea and coffee required to the gallon, see Chapter II, "Afternoon Dances."

At these entertainments a supper is given on the principle of a ball-supper, only that as regards quantities two-thirds less would be required. Thus in providing a reception-supper for 300 guests, two-thirds less would be required than for a ball-supper of the same number of guests.

A confectioner's charge for supplying an "At Home" supper, including the hire of all articles required, is from 8s. 6d. to 15s. per head, according to the description of supper ordered. As the usual dishes given at ball-suppers have been described in detail in the chapter entitled "Balls and Dances," it would be superfluous to repeat here what has already been said, and all necessary information respecting ball-suppers will be found in Chapter V.

With regard to the champagne, the quantity drunk at an "At Home" is usually one-third less than that drunk at a ball-supper. Thus the proportion of champagne drunk at an "At Home" supper would be 3½ dozen to 4 dozen to every 100 guests.

The number of waiters required at an "At Home" supper is identical with that required at a ball-supper. (See Chapter V, "Balls and Dances" on the subject of waiters and waiting.) With respect to the arrangements of the cloak-room, see chapter on "Balls and Dances."

For the cost of hire of awnings for doorways, *see* same chapter.

SMALL AT HOMES

The idea is now gradually gaining ground amongst some people that the regulation "At Home" supper is an unnecessary expense, and that guests neither require it nor care for it. They arrive from ten to eleven, thus having had ample time allowed them for dinner. They leave between twelve and one, or even earlier, and an appetite for hot soup or cold *entrées* is hardly to be acquired in the interim. Thus in some houses what are termed "light refreshments" are given during the whole of the evening, and a supper entirely dispensed with.

Again, others make a sort of compromise between no supper at all or an expensive supper, and give what is popular with the

many, a "light refection." This is served at a very small expense
it therefore enables genial, sociable people not over-burdened
with wealth to give many pleasant evening-parties at a moderate
and reasonable cost, instead of limiting their hospitality to one
expensive entertainment from which the pleasure derived by either
host or guest is totally inadequate to the cost incurred.

In giving these light suppers champagne is not even thought
of, and good hot coffee is found to be an agreeable substitute
for sherry, and although sherry and claret-cup are provided, yet
coffee is apparently preferred to either; thus the wine-bill for 100
guests assumes very modest dimensions, and does not overweigh
the expenses of the light supper itself. But few preparations are
necessary as regards arranging the drawing-room for a small "At
Home." The one aim is to gain as much space as possible, by
placing sofas, settees, and chairs, in the most convenient manner
the carpet is not covered with a dancing-cloth; floral decoration
are not attempted to any great extent. With regard to lighting the
rooms, the addition of a few wax-candles to the every-day mode of
lighting is generally considered to be sufficient for the occasion; but
ornamental candle-shades of different colours, shapes, and styles
have a pretty effect, and are now generally used.

The expense of an awning is seldom incurred, and the carriage
roller under foot and an umbrella over head are sufficient protection
even for a wet night. When light refreshments are served during the
whole of the evening, and supper not provided, they are served from
a buffet in the dining-room by the women-servants of the house; and
this plan occasions far less trouble to the giver of an entertainment
than is entailed by giving a supper on even the smallest of scales
For instance, no supper room is required, and all the preparation
attendant upon giving a supper avoided, such as the hire of plate
glass and china, lights, &c., and engaging waiters in addition to the
actual expenses of the supper itself. When only tea-room refreshments
are given, the services of two or three women-servants are sufficient in
the tea-room, according to the number of guests, and the attendance
of two men-servants in the hall and on the staircase, the one servant

to open the hall door and the other to announce the guests to the hostess at the drawing-room door.

When a light supper is given, consisting merely of sandwiches, patties, jellies, creams, &c., it is usual to serve it at twelve o'clock in the tea-room, unless found more convenient to serve it in a larger room. In providing tea-room refreshments and a light supper of the above description for 100 guests the following quantities would be found sufficient.

Tea-room refreshments.—Three gallons of coffee, 8 oz. to the gallon, best coffee at 2s. per lb.; 3 gallons of tea, 4 oz. to the gallon at 3g. 6d. per lb.; 4 quarts of hot milk; 1 quart of cream; 6 lbs. of sugar, loaf and crystallised, of which 4 lbs. would probably be used; 4 home-made cakes; Savoy-cake and almond-cake, 9d. per lb.; rice-cake, 7d. per lb.; currant-cake, 8d. per lb.; 4 dozen sponge biscuits, 6d. per dozen.

Light Supper Refreshments.—Ten plates of sandwiches of ham, potted chicken, or game, averaging 1s. per plate if made of home-made potted meat or ham; 4 dozen meat patties made of ham, chicken, game, or veal, costing, if made at home, 2s. per dozen, if bought at a confectioner's, 4s. per dozen, but as a rule, it is almost better to give an extra quantity of sandwiches, in lieu of meat patties. Unless the home cook is a superior maker of pastry, the pastry of the patties is likely to be unpleasantly hard, although the contents of the patties may be palatable enough; whereas the general complaint against the confectioner's patties is that they are all pastry and but little else.

Sponge cake with jam is an inexpensive sweet to give, and can be made at home at 15d. per lb. Three cakes weighing 1½ lb. each would be sufficient to provide.

Six quarts of jelly, 4 in moulds, and 2 served in jelly-glasses, the most inexpensive flavouring being orange, lemon, ruin, or sherry; if made at home the cost of either lemon or orange jelly would be 2s. 2d. per quart, and of jelly flavoured with either rum or wine, 2s. 6d. per quart. If bought at a confectioner's the cost is from 5s. to 7s. per mould.

Two quart-moulds of *blanc mange* would cost, if home-made, 2s. 6d. each, and 6s. each if bought at a confectioner's. In the summer months moulds of stewed fruit, stiffened with gelatine, are sometimes given, costing from 1s. to 1s. 6d. per mould. Two quart-moulds of coffee cream would cost, if home made, 2s. 6d. each, and if bought at a confectioner's the charge would be 5s. per mould.

A trifle is not a cheap dish to give, even when home-made, but it is one that is generally liked. Four trifles would be the proportion required for this number of guests, the cost of which would average 4s. each, if home-made, or from 7s. 6d. to 12s. 6d., if bought at a confectioner's.

Tipsy cake is less expensive than a trifle, costing, if home-made, 3s. a mould, and from 5s. 6d. to 7s. 6d., if bought ready made. When coffee is served during supper, 2½ gallons would be required for 100 guests; and the proportion of wine drunk would probably only average ½ a dozen bottles of sherry, and the same quantity of claret. If coffee is not given, the proportion of sherry drunk would average from 18 to 24 bottles; very good sherry may be purchased at from 36s. to 48s. per dozen. In the summer months claret cup, Badminton, or even cider-cup are refreshing, cheap, popular cups to give; and soda-water and seltzer-water should always be provided, say 3 dozen of each; but lemonade or negus are more appropriate drinks to give at juvenile parties than at evening parties.

With regard to the quantity of china, glass, and plate required for the before-mentioned number of guests the following articles would be necessary:—6 dozen forks, 2 dozen table-spoons, 3 dozen dessert-spoons, 6 dozen tea-spoons, 6 dozen wine glasses, 3 dozen tumblers, 6 dozen cups and saucers, 6 dozen supper plates. For cost of hire, see chapter on "Balls and Dances."

VII

AMATEUR THEATRICALS

Amateur Theatricals and Tableaux Vivants—Arrangements of Drawing-rooms for Theatricals—Erection of Stage—Hire of Stage accessories—Curtain, Footlights, Wings, &c.—Arrangement of Seats and hire of the same—The difficulty in distributing parts to Amateur Actors—Pieces popular with Amateurs—Tea-room Refreshments—Suppers on various scales

AMATEUR THEATRICALS AND *TABLEAUX VIVANTS* are fashionable and popular entertainments to give, and although less expensive than a ball or dance, they yet entail considerable trouble with regard to the necessary arrangements, especially to those who are amateurs in giving amateur theatricals, and it is to these that this chapter will more particularly apply. Those, however, who are in the habit of giving theatricals and who are fond of acting themselves, usually have a small theatre of their own attached to their house, and when this is the case amateur theatricals are given with as little trouble as attends the giving an ordinary evening party. Others, who have not the convenience of a theatre attached to or in the house, have a stage made to fit one of their reception-rooms, which can be put up and removed at pleasure; in addition to this they have a drop-scene, a curtain, footlights, wings, scenery, and all other necessary appliances ready for use on every occasion. Theatricals are only given by those who have a partiality for acting themselves, or when the members of their family take delight in this amusement, or in co-operation with friends who have a reputation for being talented actors. Thus, when theatricals are given by experienced amateurs accustomed to act together, the difficulty that usually attends the formation of a company is obviated, while to novices in such matters it is a very formidable affair.

As a rule the piece chosen does not at first meet with the entire

approbation of the company, each member fancying more or les
that his or her talents would be better developed in some othe
piece than the one selected. Then again, if the piece should happe
to be a manuscript one, written by an amateur, actors of hig
standing in the company object to it on the ground that being a
unpublished piece and an untried one it may not be a success o
probably never be acted again; and therefore they do not care t
learn a part which they may never be required to repeat and whic
cannot in consequence be added to their *repertoire*—they prefe
on the contrary, to draw upon the stock pieces of their youth
which only require a few hours' study in the way of refreshing thei
memory, instead of the arduous labour consequent upon learning
new part. They further object that their memory is not as retentiv
as it once was, and that they have not the leisure for careful stud
even if they had the inclination.

The memory of a professional actor is never allowed to becom
rusty through not being constantly exercised, as is too often th
memory of an amateur actor, who acts only occasionally and a
uncertain intervals. Thus, when a new piece is to be attempte
the parts should rather be offered to rising talent—whose readines
and zeal will make ample amends for lack of experience—than t
recognized stars, always taking for granted that talent is there an
only awaits a fitting opportunity for its proper development.

Again, popular amateur actors and beginners do not as a rule pu
well together, the one is apt to be a trifle supercilious to the othe
and to fear that his reputation as an actor is likely to suffer throug
the shortcomings of the company in general.

On the other hand, the name of a popular amateur actor lend
a *prestige* to a company and gives a promise of some good actin
being seen; a genial good-natured actor is often of great service i
offering suggestions to inexperienced amateurs, more especiall
to the ladies of a company, as, if he is not intimately acquainte
with the young men, he is apt to overlook and ignore them
An experienced stage manager and an intelligent prompter ar
of the greatest assistance to a young company and render the

independent of the advice of their brother actors. When amateur actors are not of the same calibre, it is often found expedient to concentrate the strength of the company upon one piece and to allot some lighter part to its subordinate members. Occasionally an amateur company is composed almost entirely of the members of one family, brothers and sisters. This has certain advantages—it affords opportunities for more frequent rehearsals; but in such a company as this there is invariably a tameness and sameness, and too close a family resemblance to offer sufficient variety or to create the illusion that the actors are other than they are, the Messrs. and the Misses Brown; the very similarity that generally exists between the voices of brothers and sisters also contributes to make the close relationship between the actors the more apparent. Thus, when possible, the family talent should be divided and varied by the introduction of a strange element, represented by friends or more distant relatives.

Concerning the choice of pieces: duet pieces, or pieces with not more than four characters are the most in favour for drawing-room acting, especially little trifles adapted from the French, which demand far less space and fewer stage accessories than do more ambitious pieces; amongst the pieces of both classes suitable to amateur actors and private theatres are the following:—

Two-Character Pieces, One Male and One Female:—"A Happy Pair;" "Husband in Clover;" "Love Test;" "Morning Call;" "Peace at any Price;" "Sympathy."

Three-Character Pieces, Two Male and One Female:—"Box and Cox;" "Cut Off with a Shilling;" "Delicate Ground;" "My Wife's Diary;" "Our Bitterest Foe;" "Ruth's Romance;" "My Aunt's Advice."

Four-Character Piece, Three Male and One Female:—"A Comical Countess."

Four-Characters, Two Male and Two Female:—"Betsy Baker;" "A Kiss in the Dark."

Five Characters, Three Male and Two Female:—"Area Belle;" "Chiselling;" "Cool as a Cucumber;" "Day After the Wedding;"

"Storm in a Tea-cup;" "To Oblige Benson;" "An Ugly Customer;" "Whitebait at Greenwich."

Four Male and One Female:—"Cup of Tea; "Two Heads Better than One."

Five-Character Pieces, Two Male and Three Female:—"Jessamy's Courtship;" "Poor Pillicoddy;" "Widow Bewitched."

Six-Character Pieces, Three Male and Three Female:—"lesson in Love;" "Little Toddlekins;" "Jacobite;" "Mrs. White;" "My Dress Boots;" "Keep your Temper."

Six-Character Pieces, Four Male and Two Female:—"Alone;" "B. B.;" "Nursey Chickweed;" "Rough Diamond;" "Real and Ideal;" "Mode Husband."

Six-Character Pieces, Five Male and One Female:—"Blow in the Dark;" "Good for Nothing;" "Retained for the Defence."

Six-Character Pieces, Four Male and Two Female:—"Family Jars."

Seven-Character Pieces, Four Male and Three Female:—"Dearest Mamma;" "Nine Points of the Law;" "Woodcock's Little Game;" "Creatures of Impulse;" "Just my Luck;" " Little Rebel."

Seven-Character Pieces, Five Male and Two Female:—"Chimney Corner;" "First Night;" "Loan of a Lover;" "Separate Maintenance;" "Spectre Bridegroom."

Seven-Character Piece, Three Male and Four Female:—"Ici on parle Français."

Seven-Character Pieces, Six Male and One Female:—"Diamond Cut Diamond;" "Thrice Married."

Eight-Character Piece, Four Male and Four Female:—"Boots at the Swan."

Eight-Character Pieces, Five Male and Three Female:—"Little Treasure;" "Meg's Diversion."

Nine-Character Pieces, Five Male and Four Female:—"Pygmalion and Galatea;" "War to the Knife."

Six Male and Three Female:—"Bamboozling;" "Birthplace of Podgers;" "Shipmates."

Nine-Character Pieces, Seven Male and Two Female:—"Next of Kin;" "Paul Pry;" "Raising the Wind;" "Plot and Passion."

Nine-Character Pieces, Eight Male and One Female:—"To Paris and Back for £5."

Ten-Character Pieces, Five Male and Five Female:—"Cricket on the Hearth."

Ten-Character Pieces, Six Male and Four Female:—"Our Boys."

Ten-Character Pieces, Seven Male and Three Female:—"Elixir of Love;" "Helping Hands."

Eleven-Character Pieces, Seven Male and Four Female:—"The Lady of Lyons;" "Partners for Life."

Twelve-Character Pieces, Eight Male and Four Female:—"The Rivals;" "A Scrap of Paper."

Twelve-Character Pieces, Nine Male and Three Female:—"Still Waters Run Deep;" "Ticket of Leave Man."

"The School for Scandal;" and "She Stoops to Conquer," are ambitious pieces, but are often played by amateurs. In the former there are twenty-two characters, sixteen Male and six Female; in the latter, twenty characters, sixteen Male and four Female. Robertson's plays are all popular with amateurs; "School," "Caste," and "Society," are especially so.

The pieces here given are all well-known to play goers, and it is perhaps for this reason that amateur actors prefer them for representation; they have seen them acted either in public or in private and are able to judge which parts are most suited to their capabilities, while the pieces themselves possess such intrinsic merit that even when most indifferently acted, they command the interest of the audience which a mediocre piece, under similar circumstances, would fail to secure. Thus amateur actors run the gauntlet of unfavourable comparison, and chance the intimate acquaintance of their audience with the piece chosen rather than not produce a well-known favourite.

A book of any published play can be ordered through a bookseller, or direct from Mr. French, late Lacy, theatrical bookseller, Strand, at the cost of from 6d. to 1s. each, but there are certain pieces of which the "Acting Right" is retained, and for which a fee must be paid for permission to play; the fee varies from 7s. 6d. to 21s., according to whether the piece chosen is a one, three, four or five act play, or whether it has been performed in London or in the provinces only.

All stage scenery can be hired—such as back scenes, borders and sides, interiors, exteriors, streets, mountain scenery, ruins, roadside inns, &c.—and the hire of these appliances is comparatively moderate, but amateurs who are capable of painting their own scenes generally do so, as it comes much less expensive than the constant hire of scenery, and miniature designs for the assistance of the amateur scene-painter can be purchased, at a cost of from 6d. to 1s.

The hire of foot-lights is from 6d. to 9d. per lamp, but these again are oftener purchased than hired as the original outlay is but a small one.

The hire of a curtain ranges from £1 1s. and upwards.

For the representation of *tableaux vivants* the same stage accessories are usually employed as for amateur theatricals. The choice of *tableaux* embraces a wide range of subjects, including the literature of many periods, both prose and poetry, in addition to the well-known works of popular R.A.'s, which latter are very favourite studies for *tableaux vivants*.

Amateur theatricals or *tableaux vivants* last from two to three hours, according to length of the pieces or the number of the *tableaux* chosen.

It is usual to invite the guests half-an-hour previous to the rising of the curtain, that the audience may be seated, in order to avoid any interruption during the performance; thus, if the curtain were to rise at half-past nine, nine would be the hour named on the invitation card; if at nine, half-past eight would be the hour named, the latter hour being, perhaps, more usual in the country and at watering-places and suburban towns than in town during the season, when receptions are given at the latest possible hours for the convenience of the guests.

The usual seats provided for guests at these entertainments are cane or rush-seated chairs, which are placed in rows and fastened together. The cost of hire of these chairs averages from 4s. to 6s. per dozen.

The guests on their arrival are ushered to the cloak-room as at an evening party. For the arrangements of the cloak-room, see Chapter V, "Balls and Dances."

The light refreshments necessary for an entertainment of this description are similar in all respects to those provided for an evening reception, and the same quantities would be requisite in proportion to the numbers invited.

Tea is served in the tea-room to the guests on their arrival, and again in the interval between the first and second piece, or between the first and second set of *tableaux*. For cost and quantities see Chapter VI, entitled "Receptions, &c.;" where also the supper arrangements are given.

A supper given at an entertainment of this character is carried out on the same scale as one given at a small reception or "At Home," or even on a smaller scale, such as the following, which is an inexpensive and suitable supper to provide when it is desirable to keep down the expenses as far as possible. An inexpensive supper for fifty guests, might include the following:—

10 lbs. of glazed beef, at 8d. per lb., allowing 1s. for flavouring and glazing.

Two tongues, glazed, weighing 5 lb. per tongue.

Four cold roast chickens, 5s. 6d. the couple; these should be carved ready for helping and tied into shape again with ribbon before being sent to table. Chickens cut up and tied into shape have a more tempting appearance than when palpably cut into portions. Uncut chickens necessitate a carver possessing some little experience in the art of carving, otherwise he may make sad havoc of a chicken and give but a sorry help to the lady he has taken down to supper; whereas, when chicken or pheasant is carved in the kitchen many more good helps can be had from a couple of birds than if the helping depends upon the skill of an hap-hazard carver; as a rule eight helps may be obtained from an average-sized chicken, as, contrary to dinner, at supper a leg of a chicken is considered a satisfactory help.

A ham weighing 16 lbs. at 11d. per lb.

Meat-pies made of beef-steak or veal and ham, are not much fancied at supper, and are, therefore, but seldom given: there is an idea that these pies are more or less indigestible; but an exception is made in favour of pigeon-pie, although it is not an economical dish to give.

The cost of salad depends upon the season of the year: sufficient for two bowls of salad would average from 3s. to 4s. 6d. the bowl, including eggs and dressing, if made at home. At all suppers, large or small, salad is invariably given, as it is a necessary adjunct to cold chicken, ham, tongue, &c. Especial care should be taken that the salad is fresh and crisp, and that it is dressed after a good recipe; vinegar, used with discretion, and pure oil instead of strong oil, and that the cream should not be forgotten. Further, when *ordering* a salad it is as well to remind the greengrocer not to fill up the basket with mustard and cress, which is the least desirable portion of a salad, and to throw in a *soupçon* of tarragon or chervil in addition to the lettuce, endive, beet-root, &c.

Tasty sandwiches made of potted game, potted meat, or potted fish, are generally liked; the cost of these would average 2s. per dish: three dishes would be a fair proportion to give.

The sweets given, at this style of supper would comprise 4 jellies, flavoured with liqueur; the cost of these, if home made, would amount to 2s. 6d. per mould.

A trifle, also made at home, would cost 5s. 6d.

2 jam sponge-cakes, home made, 1s. 6d. the cake.

2 moulds of fruit costing from 1s. 6d. to 2s. per mould.

2 dishes of tartlets at the cost of 1s. 6d. per dish.

1 or 2 *blanc manges*, or the same number of coffee creams, are inexpensive sweets to give.

3 or 4 dishes of fruit are usually given; in the winter, oranges, pears, &c., in the summer season, strawberries, grapes, or peaches, &c.

It is found a very economical plan to serve good hot coffee during supper, as the guests often prefer it to sherry or claret. When coffee is given 2 dozen bottles of wine would be required, 1 dozen of sherry and 1 dozen of claret, and probable only two-thirds of this quantity would be drunk; 2 dozen of seltzer-water would be provided at 1s. 6d. per dozen.

Sherry at 48s. per dozen is an average price to give, while Crown champagne at 42s. per dozen is not unfrequently given by those who cannot afford and are not expected to offer a better class of wine; 2 dozen of champagne would be the probable quantity drunk by the before-mentioned number of guests.

VIII

JUVENILE PARTIES

Juvenile Parties—Amusements suitable for Juvenile Parties—The expense of hire of Special Amusements—Suitable pieces for Juvenile Amateurs.—The quantities required for Juvenile Teas—Arrangements of the Tea-table—Light Refreshments—Light Suppers.

CHILDREN'S PARTIES ARE GIVEN MORE or less throughout the year. In the winter months the amusements provided take place within doors, in the summer months they are held out of doors; but as a rule the children of every household are indulged with one, if not with many, juvenile parties during the year. Parties are given on a large or small scale, according to the inclination of parents, ranging from a simple little party of six children, to a fancy dress-ball of ninety or one hundred children.

The season of Christmas is, however, the season of all others when children's parties on a large scale are at their height.

Four hours are the usual limits of a child's party, and it is injudicious to attempt to crowd too great a variety of amusements into this space of time, as the programme must, in such a case, be hurriedly gone through to be fully completed before the hour of departure.

Afternoon juvenile parties take place from 4 to 7; evening juvenile parties from 6 to 10.

It is usual to provide some special amusement for children apart from games and dancing.

The "conjuror" is always in request, and the charge for an exhibition of conjuring for either afternoon or evening parties varies according to circumstances from one to five guineas.

In town the newest amusements are readily obtainable, in

addition to such old favourites as Marionnettes, Punch and Judy, Performing Dogs, Performing Birds, &c., &c. The cost of hire of either of the above ranges from two to ten guineas.

Those who do not wish to go to the expense of providing any especial amusement for children, exercise their own ingenuity in organising some home amusement, and in spending in small Christmas presents money that would otherwise be expended in the hire of a performing *troupe*. Christmas-trees are now quite out of date in the drawing-room, and have been succeeded by other devices for the distribution of presents, though it is doubtful if any innovation will afford as much pleasure to children as a well-laden, well-lighted Christmas-tree has been wont to do.

Old Father Christmas with a lucky bag; Santa Claus with a stocking of monster dimensions; a Yule log decorated and stuffed with presents; fishing for presents in a Fairy Well—constructed in a back drawing-room—are a few of the many mediums resorted to at Christmas for the amusement of children and the distribution of presents. As to the expense incurred by giving Christmas presents, it naturally depends upon the pockets and positions of the parents of the children; some providing beautiful presents and others giving merely the most inexpensive and homely ones.

Presents, however small, run into a certain sum of money, and £5 is very soon spent in this way, and those who do not wish to run into any avoidable expense when giving a children's party, do not attempt providing Christmas presents for little guests. A pre-arranged charade with grotesque costumes acted by the members of the family, or even a little fairy piece acted by the children of the family, are popular and inexpensive diversions at children's parties, or *tableaux vivants* from well-known nursery rhymes; or fairy tales excite no little wonder and pleasure amongst juvenile audiences, and give considerable gratification to the young performers themselves.

Amongst popular plays for children are the following:—

"Beauty and the Beast," (8 characters); "Blue Beard," (11 characters); "The White Cat," (9 characters); "Cinderella," (9 characters); "The Yellow Dwarf," (12 characters); "Aladdin," (11 characters); "Puss in Boots," (17 characters); "Little Red Riding-Hood," (13 characters); "The Sleeping Beauty," (13 characters); "Ali Baba," (9 characters); "Fairyland," (9 characters); "Jack and the Beanstalk," (5 characters); "King Alfred and the Cakes," (7 characters.)

Musical Plays.—"Ten Tortured Tutors," (10 characters); "School Bor-ed," (5 characters); "Of Noble Birth," (4 characters); "Pills of Wisdom," (13 characters); "Dr. Barlow," (12 characters.)

Burlesques.—"The Blazing Burgee," (4 characters); "The Port Admiral," (5 characters); "Briganzio the Brigand," (4 characters); "The Tyrant, the Slave, the Victim, and the Tar," (5 characters); "The Rosebud of Stinging Nettle Farm," (5 characters); "Stirring the Pudding," (6 characters); "Compliments of the Season," (5 characters); "The King of the Bean," (8 characters.)

Charade Plays.—"Blue Beard," (8 characters); "Phaeton," (8 characters); "Cataline," (11 characters); "Guy Faux," (9 characters); "Counterplot," (9 characters); "Blindfold," (8 characters); "Outlaw," (7 characters); "Sleeping Draught," (7 characters.)

Boisterous games or games in which children of all ages can join never fail to amuse; but it is generally found that if prolonged beyond an hour, the younger children become tired and cross, the older boys obstreperous and unmanageable, while the little girls either loudly complain of the rough play of the boys, or take refuge in tears, at which the mammas present are very much concerned. Thus games, to be a success, require to be put an end to at the first indication of either weariness or roughness, and a quiet amusement substituted.

It much depends upon the ages of the children whether dancing is the chief feature at a juvenile party, or whether it is only limited to one hour. If the majority of the children are boys, they prefer any description of amusement to dancing; if the contrary is the case the little girls are generally found willing to dance as long as any one is willing to play for them. Generally the governess, or one of the members of the family undertakes the musical arrangements, otherwise a professional pianist is engaged to play the piano; the cost of whose services averages from 15s. to 1 guinea. A piano is considered sufficient at juvenile parties without the addition of any other instrument.

Soon after the arrival of children at a juvenile party, they are taken down into the dining-room to have tea; if space permits, seats are provided for all; if not, the earliest arrivals are sent in to tea without delay, and are followed in their turn by later arrivals.

For a party of fifty children the following quantities would be consumed:—1 gallon of tea; from ½ a gallon to 1 gallon of coffee—allowing 4 oz, of tea at 3s. per lb. to the gallon; and 6 oz. of coffee, at 1s. 10d. per lb. to the gallon. Hot and cold milk, 5 quarts, allowing 2½ quarts to the gallon, at from 4d. to 5d. per quart.

Of sugar, 4 lbs. would be provided, at 5d. per lb and 3 lbs. would probably be consumed.

Twelve plates of thin bread and butter, allowing 2 quartern loaves, and 2 lbs. of butter at 1s. 6d. per lb.

Three plum or currant cakes weighing 2 lbs. each, home-made, at 8d. per lb.

Two rice-cakes, same weight, home-made, 7d. per lb.; 4 lbs. of various kinds of biscuits at from 6d. to 8d. per lb.; 2½ dozen sponge-cakes, home-made, 6d. per dozen, or, if bought at a confectioner's, 1s. per dozen.

Four dozen small buns at 6d. per dozen.

When fruit is not in season, preserve or honey is often given at a children's tea-party, either strawberry, raspberry, or gooseberry jam; 4 lbs. of jam at 9d. per lb. would be sufficient to provide. When fresh fruit is given, either strawberries, raspberries, or currants, 10 or 12 lbs. would be the proportion. Fruit is eaten after bread and butter and cake. The cost of fruit averages from 6d. to 9d. per lb.; when at a higher price it is not often given at children's parties.

The number of cups and saucers required for a party of these dimensions would be 5 dozen, a few extra being required for those ladies who accompany the children into the tea-room. The hire of cups and saucers is 9d. per dozen; 5 dozen tea-spoons would also be required. The hire of tea-spoons is 1s. 6d. per dozen; dessert-spoons for jam, 2 dozen would be required; small bread and butter plates, 5 dozen, the hire of these is 1s. per dozen.

The tea-table should be entirely covered with a white table-cloth. Tea and coffee and tea-cups are placed on a tea-tray at either end, and dishes of eatables are placed down the centre of the table.

The governess of the family, assisted by one or more of the grown-up daughters, pours out the tea and coffee, and the women-servants are in attendance to supply the children with all they may require, overlooked and assisted by the ladies present.

The light refreshments usually provided for children at a juvenile evening party are served twice during the evening, that is to say, an hour after tea, and an hour before leaving; they principally consist of dessert in the winter season, such as oranges, figs, almonds and raisins, and French plums. On Twelfth Night, a twelfth-cake is always provided in addition to sponge cakes, almond cakes, and plum cakes. Lemonade, orangeade, wine-and-water, or homemade wine, are the description of drinks supplied.

The quantity of dessert necessary for a party of fifty children would average as follows:—

Four and a half dozen of dessert oranges at from 10d. to 1s. per dozen; 3 lbs. of figs at 6d. per lb.; 3 lbs. of dessert raisins at 1s. per lb.; 1½ lbs. of almonds at 1s. 2d. per lb.; 3 lbs. of French plums at 1s. 4d. per lb.

Three dozen costume crackers at 2s. per dozen.

The cost of a twelfth-cake, made at home, sufficiently rich for children, including icing, would amount to 1s. per lb. A 4-lb. cake would be a reasonable sized cake. When twelfth-cake is not given, 2 sponge cakes and 2 plum cakes, weighing 3 lbs. each, would be cut up into small pieces; 6 lbs. of each description of cake would be sufficient. If homemade, the cost of either would be 8d. per lb. 4 lbs. of fancy biscuits, at 1s. per lb., would also be required.

For mixing wine and water, 3 bottles of sherry, at 36s. per doz., would be a fair quantity, in addition to 6 quarts of orange and lemonade, allowing 1 doz. lemons, at 1s. 4d. per doz., or bottles of lemon-juice, at 6d. per bottle, for making 3 quarts of lemonade, in addition to 3 lbs. of white sugar, at 5d. per lb., and for orangeade, 2 doz. oranges, at 8d. per doz., and 3 lbs. of sugar, at 5d. per lb.

At some children's parties orange wine and ginger wine are given in place of sherry and water; 4 bottles of British wine, at the cost of 1s. 2d. per bottle, would probably be drunk.

It is not always that this class of dessert, or any class of dessert, is provided at a children's party, and people frequently consider that a glass of wine and water or lemonade and a piece of cake on departure is all that children require after a good tea, but if the generality of children were consulted there would not be a doubt as to their opinion about it.

When a juvenile party is given, from 25 to 30 grown-up people are usually asked—the relatives of the children—who either accompany them or arrive shortly after tea, and for whom a small supper is provided, served at half-past seven, before the departure of the children, or in the evening after their dispersal. An inexpensive class of supper will be found described at page 107.

Part II

IX

BREAKFAST PARTIES

*The Expenses attendant upon giving Breakfast Parties of various dimensions—
Breakfasts in Town—The importance of a pleasant Breakfast-room—Varieties
of Breakfast Dishes from which to select—The cost thereof—Country house
Breakfasts—Country prices versus Town—Hunt Breakfasts—Their mode of
Arrangement—The Order of Viands given and the Quantities for a given
number—Bachelors' Breakfasts.*

THERE IS NO MEAL ABOUT which so great a diversity of opinion
exists as "breakfast," and respecting which such perfect
freedom is accorded by general consent. The hour itself is an elastic
one, stretching from eight to twelve, as individual convenience
dictates. Business men breakfast from eight to nine; professional
men breakfast at nine; those who are neither professional men nor
business men are partial to the hour of ten, while young men who
live in chambers and who keep late hours, think eleven or twelve a
very reasonable hour at which to breakfast.

The family breakfast hour is regulated in a great measure by
the pursuits of the family; nine is a very general hour, and ten is
perhaps an equally general one, but with a scintillation of fashion
surrounding it which nine does not possess.

Breakfast is popularly supposed to be the most sociable of meals, but
whether it is so or not entirely depends upon the disposition of those
assembled at breakfast; some people are at their best at this meal, and
others at their worst; some are bright and cheery, others morose and
silent. The morning's letters or the quotations of the Money Market in

the morning's papers are responsible for much of this fluctuation, while health and temper are perhaps answerable for the rest.

Although punctuality on the part of guests with regard to their coming down to breakfast is not compulsory, it is yet more courteous to the host and hostess and more conducive to the comfort of the guests themselves when some regard is paid to the sound of the breakfast gong; and though a host and hostess do not wait breakfast for their guests, it yet appears unsociable to sit down to table without them, and a hostess who is solicitous for the *bien être* of her guests, is vexed when everything is half-cold before their entrance. The eight o'clock cup of tea sent to the members of a family, and to their guests, is so usual an attention, and is so appreciated by all, that none but the most economical and penurious of housekeepers attempt to dispense with it, the cost being of so trifling a character.

A pleasant breakfast-room is a great acquisition to a house. In town, space does not often admit of this luxury, and the dining-room serves as breakfast-room, but in the country some bright room, having a southern aspect, is denominated the breakfast-room, simply furnished with light inexpensive furniture, and partaking of the character of half boudoir, half dining-room, being neither so richly furnished as the one nor so solidly furnished as the other, and used as an occasional sitting-room when required.

In town houses, where the dining-room is the family breakfast-room, it is important that the windows should be opened at an early hour in the morning, not later than seven, in order that fresh air may freely circulate through the room, to divest it of the odours of the dinner of the previous evening and of the close air engendered by gas, where gas is used. Servants are not, as a rule, sufficiently thoughtful in the matter of airing the dining-room, and do not estimate the difference between a fresh atmosphere and a close, oppressive one. The breakfast appetites of those who reside in town are proverbially smaller and less robust than of those who reside in the country; late hours and heated rooms on the one hand, and early hours and fresh country air on the other, are doubtless responsible for this difference, and for the contrast that the town breakfast table offers to the country breakfast table, besides which the home farm and the home preserves provide luxuriously for the one, while the other has no such resource at command, and every article placed upon its swells the household bills in a larger or smaller degree. Those who reside in country and seaside towns, or in the suburbs of London, find a like difficulty in supplying the breakfast table as regards variety and cost. What to order for breakfast is a problem that puzzles many young housekeepers with whom economy is more or less an object. "Eggs and bacon" is oftener than not the only dish that suggests itself to the mind of the inexperienced housekeeper, but this dish represents neither economy nor variety; its one merit is perhaps that it suits all palates, and that frequent repetition does not produce satiety, as is the case with most other dishes. The cost, in town, of what are termed new-laid eggs, averages from 3d. to 4d. each, while breakfast bacon averages from 10d. to 14d. per lb.; thus the cost of a dish of eggs and bacon sufficient for eight people would amount to 3s. 6d. In frying bacon the waste is considerable, but by far the most palatable manner of cooking bacon, as well as the most economical, is to toast it in a Dutch oven before the fire, or to broil it on a gridiron over a clear fire.

Many heads of households have a rooted objection to that much abused culinary article, the frying-pan; while indifferent cooks entertain a decided partiality for it, and lamb chops, kidneys, and rashers of bacon are indiscriminately sacrificed to it. Thus the ubiquitous dish of eggs and bacon is, thanks to the frying-pan, not always the delicacy requisite to tempt fastidious appetites, and a dish of toasted bacon and poached eggs, puts a dish of fried bacon with its setting of half cold fat and suspicious-looking eggs to the blush.

New-laid eggs, when boiled, are often sent up to table wrapped in a well-warmed *serviette* on a well-warmed dish, that they may be kept hot until they are eaten, instead of being placed in an egg-stand, where they soon become cold.

For a party of eight, from 8 to 10 boiled eggs would be an average proportion. Sausages are an economical breakfast dish, approved of by some and disapproved of by others; 2 lbs. of Cambridge sausages, at 1s. to 1s. 2d. per lb., is a sufficiently large dish for eight people, in addition to other things.

Devilled kidneys are much given for breakfast; 10 kidneys at 4d. each would make a fair-sized dish for eight people.

Broiled chicken is a good breakfast dish, the price of it depending upon the season of the year, and the size of the fowl; from April to July an average-sized chicken may be had from 3s. to 4s. 6d., and from July to March at from 2s. 9d. to 3s. 6d. Again, when a pair of chickens have formed part of the dinner of the previous evening, sufficient is often left to make a dish of broil for breakfast, in which case the cost of such a dish would be but one-fourth of the original price. A broil is very dependent upon the nature of the sauce served with it. If served without a piquant sauce it is a dry joke, and every good housekeeper has her especial recipe for a famous sauce.

Lamb chops and mutton chops are more affected by bachelors than by heads of families, as they form a rather substantial breakfast dish—too substantial for ladies to indulge in thus early in the day. For a party of eight—four ladies and four gentlemen—6 mutton or lamb chops would be the proportion; which dish would average from 3s. 6d. to 4s. 6d. It is needless to say that to suit the masculine taste these chops should be broiled on a gridiron and served *without* sauce.

Broiled rump-steak with mushrooms is rather a bachelor's than a family breakfast dish; 2½ lbs. of steak at 1s. 4d. per lb. and 1½ lbs. of mushrooms at 1s. per lb. would be a fair-sized dish for a party of eight. Here, again, the gridiron should "oust" the frying-pan; indeed, it is a grave question whether, in the interest of breakfast, an indifferent cook should be trusted with the possession of a frying-pan, or whether it should not be put under lock and key while the preparations for the morning meal are going on.

Kippered-salmon, kippered-herrings, bloaters, and dried haddocks are economical and favourite breakfast dishes; the cost of which for eight people would average from 2s. to 5s., according to the fish selected.

Fresh herrings, when in season, are cheap and palatable.

Broiled salmon as a breakfast dish is also much appreciated by men.

Broiled soles make a good breakfast dish, and average from 1s. 6d. to 3s. per pair, as do mackerel and whiting.

Dressed fish is a popular breakfast dish, and anything but an expensive one, as it is usually made of fish left from the dinner of the previous evening. Either cod, turbot, or brill, is the best fish for this purpose.

Broiled mushrooms are often given for breakfast, and, when in season, the cost of a fair-sized dish for eight people, would be from 2s. to 3s. 6d.

Potatoes are given for breakfast with sausages or with rump-steak, either mashed or broiled.

A savoury omelette is a tasty breakfast dish; the cost of which for eight persons would be about 2s. 6d.

Buttered eggs for eight people would cost about the same.

A good supply of cold meats, &c., is usually provided in addition to hot things; but when a breakfast-party principally consists of ladies, very little cold meat is eaten, and, therefore, but little is provided, and eggs and bacon or fish are the dishes most in favour with them. The supply on the side-table is, therefore, regulated according to the number of gentlemen present at breakfast.

Some men prefer breakfasting off cold roast beef to other cold meat, and in households where this taste is encouraged, the joint of roast beef sent up to dinner the day previous is placed on the side-table for breakfast.

A leg or loin of cold roast pork is also with some men a popular breakfast dish.

Cold mutton is not eaten for breakfast, and cold chicken is considered equally insipid.

Cold ham is almost a regulation breakfast dish. The average cost of ham is from 10d. to 1s. per lb. Small hams, at from 8 to

10 lbs. in weight, are not profitable, as they run very lean. Thus a medium weight—14 to 16 lbs.—is a more useful size to select for the breakfast-table, and for a party of eight each morning's consumption of ham would average from 3s. to 4s. Grated ham, ham toast, or ham omelette, are often made from the fag-end of a ham.

By far the best manner of cooking a ham is to bake it. The ham should be covered with a flour-and-water crust, and baked, according to weight, in a moderately hot oven. Cooked in this way its flavour is enhanced; it does not become hard or dry, and there is no waste: consequently, those who have given this method a trial are not likely to return to the boiling process.

Cold tongue is occasionally provided for breakfast. The cost of a tongue is from 4s. 6d. and upwards, according to weight, and for a breakfast-party of eight a fair-sized tongue would appear on the sideboard at least two mornings, and would thus cost from 2s. 6d. to 3s. 6d. per breakfast.

Brawn or collared head is often given for breakfast in the winter months. The cost ranges from 1s. to 1s. 6d. per lb., when not made at home, but if home-cured and home-made the cost is from 6d. to 9d. per lb.

Spiced beef is a substantial side-table dish, and costs, if home-made, from 8d. to 9d. per lb.

Veal-and-ham pie, pigeon pie, rabbit pie, and boned eel pie, find a place amongst other cold things on the side-table. The cost of either of these varies from 4s. and upwards, according to size, and a fair-sized pie would be sent in for breakfast two or three mornings, if its appearance has not been spoilt by too many attacks upon it.

The cost of a game pie, when bought, varies from 7s. 6d. to a guinea, according to size, while to buy game for the purpose of making a pie for breakfast is rather an expensive thing to do, and when game pies are made at home in town it may be taken for granted that the game has been sent by a friend and not purchased from a poulterer.

Cold pheasants, partridges, and grouse are much appreciated for breakfast; when purchased the average cost of pheasants and grouse is from 7s. to 9s. a brace, partridges from 4s. 6d. to 6s. a brace.

For a party of 8 people 1½ lb. of butter would be sent to table, and probably under 1 lb. consumed; butter is reckoned more appetizing when made into pats than when sent up in ½ lb. rolls.

Home-made potted game and potted meats are much liked for breakfast in the winter months; but tins of potted meat and fish would not be given by a considerate hostess to her guests.

Fruit is much given in the summer months, while preserves are given at all seasons of the year. Orange, quince, and apricot marmalade and honey, the cost of either of these ranges from 5d. to 8d. per lb. Muffins and buttered toast are usually given for breakfast in the winter months, and cost from 8d. to 1s. per dish. French rolls and scones are given in addition to fancy bread.

The quantity of tea and coffee to provide for a party of 8 people would be 2 quarts of tea and 2 quarts of coffee, allowing 2 ozs. of tea to 1 quart of water, and the same quantity of coffee to the quart.

The tea would only be made as required, and probably less than 2 quarts drunk, and therefore less than 4 ozs. used.

Tea at 2s. 6d. per lb. and coffee at 2s. per lb. would be an average quality to use, the cost of tea and coffee at this price would amount to 1s. 1½d. per morning.

One quart of hot milk would be the proportion to this quantity of coffee, and half a pint of cream and 1 pint of cold milk to the tea. The price of milk in town is 5d. per quart, and the price of cream is 4s. per quart. Both crystalized and loaf sugar would be provided, 1 lb. of each being the proportion. The breakfast cover for each person consists of 2 small knives, 2 small forks, a plate, and a *serviette*. The breakfast cups and saucers are placed at the top of the table before the mistress of the house with the breakfast service. (*See* the "Management of Servants.") The rolls and fancy bread, the muffin dish, the butter dish, the glass dishes of preserves, the sardines, the toast-racks with dry toast, are placed upon the table, and the hot and cold viands on the side-table, with hot and cold plates. The hot things are served on hot-water or spirit-lamp breakfast-dishes, either of silver, electro-plate or china.

BACHELORS' BREAKFASTS

The cost of bachelors' breakfast parties is arrived at by the number of guests entertained, and by the quality and variety of the dishes given.

Bachelors' breakfast parties are usually given from 11 to 12, and expense is a secondary consideration with these hosts, if a consideration at all—to have every thing earliest in season is the prevailing idea. Lamb cutlets or lamb chops when lamb is at 1s. 6d. or 2s. per lb.; broiled salmon, when salmon is at 4s. 6d. per lb.; oysters at 3s. per doz.; plovers' eggs at 6s. or 8s. per doz.; spring chickens, when chickens are 9s. 6d. per couple; whitebait, at 4s. per quart; *pâté de foie gras*, at 2 guineas the *pâté*, and so on.

At these breakfasts good claret is generally given rather than champagne, in addition to tea, coffee, and liqueurs. Champagne is principally given by young men who have not learnt to appreciate good claret. Many of the breakfast dishes enumerated in this chapter are also given, on these occasions.

COUNTRY HOUSE BREAKFASTS

The cost of country-house breakfasts differs materially from those of town breakfasts; every country gentleman estimates that there is a saving of 15 per cent, on farm produce, as compared with town prices, and this accounts in some measure for the prodigality of the country-house breakfast-table over the London breakfast-table.

In September hot roast partridges or hot roast grouse are given for breakfast, and from November to January hot roast pheasants and woodcocks, the cost being a nominal one, entirely depending upon whether an owner preserves highly, moderately, or not at all.

Hams and prime breakfast bacon, can be supplied to the house at 7½d. per lb., including the curing; chickens at the rate of 6d. to 10d. per pound on an average all the year round. Turkeys at about the same price per lb.

New laid eggs, from October to February, average 10d. a dozen; and from February to September, 6d. a dozen.

The cost of home-made sausages averages from 6d. to 7d. per lb.

The cost of fresh butter is, in the winter months, from 1s. 4d. to 2s. per pound, and in the summer months, 1s. to 1s. 7d. per lb.

New milk averages 2½d. to 3d. per quart, and cream 3s. per quart; but prices vary in different counties, and according to the time of year. In the eastern counties, for instance, all farm produce costs more in the production than is the case in the southern and western counties, and prices in the southern counties range still lower during the summer months than those above quoted.

In small households, where the consumption of farm produce is comparatively slight, there is little appreciable saving in home production, taking into account the attendant outlay, risk, and trouble.

The general cost of country produce is thus indicated to serve as a guide as to the average cost of a country breakfast, and this is regulated by the number of persons present at breakfast, and by the extent of the dishes given. A country-house breakfast sometimes includes from ten to thirty guests. The side-table on these occasions is always well-supplied with cold meat, game, &c., and two to four breakfast *entrées* are usually given.

HUNT BREAKFASTS

A Hunt Breakfast partakes of the character of a cold luncheon on a large scale, with the addition of tea and coffee, wines and liqueurs. These breakfasts are given during the hunting season by the master of the hounds, by the members of the hunt, or by any county gentleman, near whose residence the meet takes place, and who is hospitable enough to throw open his house to all comers, as it is an understood thing that the field generally are welcome at the breakfast, whether acquainted with the giver or not. No invitations are issued for these breakfasts beyond those contained in the general notice given by the M. F. H. respecting the meets of the current week.

These breakfasts are given at the expense of the host of the day, and are entirely apart from the expenses of the hunt. The guests generally average from 40 to 100, including members of the hunt and non-members, gentlemen and farmers, residents and strangers.

The breakfast is given in the large dining-room, great hall, or billiard-room, according to the accommodation required, one long table occupies the centre of the room. Breakfast-covers are placed the length of the table; a knife and fork and plate to each cover, and as each place is vacated, a fresh cover is placed in readiness for a new comer. Ladies are seldom present at hunt breakfasts, and those who ride or drive to the meet, and are acquainted with the lady of the house where a breakfast is given, are ushered on their arrival into the drawing-room or morning-room, where refreshments are offered them, tea, coffee, sherry, sandwiches, cake, &c.

9.30 to 10 is the time usually fixed for a hunt breakfast, although this is regulated by the hour at which the hounds are to meet. At hunt breakfasts hot *entrées* are not given; a large supply of cold viands is necessary; cold beef is the *pièce de resistance* at these entertainments, as the hunting farmers prefer something substantial to commence upon.

Twenty to thirty lbs. of sirloin or corned beef is usually provided. Very few squires kill their own beef, and the cost of either fresh beef or salt beef, if purchased of a country butcher, averages from 10d. to 11d. per lb.

The probable number of those who are likely to attend a hunt breakfast is generally known by the giver, and breakfast is provided in accordance with the number of guests expected.

For 30 guests the following supply would be a fair proportion:

A sirloin, or round of beef weighing from 16 lbs., at 10d. to 11d. per lb.

A ham, weighing 16 lbs., at 1s. per lb., or 7d. per lb. if home cured.

One ox-tongue, weighing 7 lbs., at 1s. per lb., or 9d. per lb. if home cured.

Cold roast pheasants or game pie; roast chickens or roast turkey would also be given; and as this game and poultry would be furnished from the home preserves and home farm, the cost would be considerably under market price.

A piece of cheese, weighing from 12 lbs. to 15 lbs. would be provided, either Cheddar or North Wiltshire, the cost of which would amount to 9d. or 10d. per lb., as bread and cheese is in great demand at hunt breakfasts.

All the cold meats, game, &c., are placed on the breakfast-table, and the guests help themselves to what they require. As a rule gentlemen eat but little at hunt breakfasts, and breakfast at home before starting; farmers, on the contrary, make a hearty meal, having perhaps breakfasted at a much earlier hour. A host, when ordering a hunt breakfast, takes into consideration the class of guests he expects, and regulates the supply according to the probable demand.

Sherry, brandy, cherry-brandy, liqueurs, and ale, are always provided. Champagne is only occasionally given.

The proportion of wine drunk by 30 guests would be of sherry under three bottles; of brandy under two bottles; of cherry-brandy under two bottles. Of ale two gallons would be drawn, if not drunk.

X

LUNCHEON PARTIES

The Cost of giving Luncheon Parties—Large Luncheons—Small Luncheons—Favourite Luncheon Dishes—The Proportion to provide for a given number of Guests—Luncheon Menus

L UNCHEON IS IN SOME HOUSES a sort of "open house" hospitality to which intimate friends of the family are expected to drop in without invitation and without ceremony. Where this custom is established much geniality and sociability prevails, as guests who are thus privileged to present themselves in this unceremonious manner at a luncheon table are, as a matter of course, very much at home at a house, and on the friendliest footing with its master and mistress.

In addition to the general invitations thus given to luncheon, when it is uncertain whether any or many will appear, it is customary to invite less intimate friends on three or four days during a week, say two or three guests each day.

The practice of this hospitality naturally entails an increase of expenditure, and there are various ways of providing for this class of luncheon, one being to do things well and liberally, and another to study economy in every detail, bringing the expenses within the smallest possible limits. To follow that first-mentioned is easy enough, income permitting, when it resolves itself into a mere question of what to have and what to order; but the second requires intelligence, method and experience, and there are many clever and careful housekeepers whose incomes do not admit of much outlay in this direction, but who yet give good luncheons at a very moderate cost, and whose "luncheon table" is a favourite and pleasant resort for their friends; these hospitable people seldom lunch *en famille*, others on the contrary, do not give general invitations to luncheon, but entertain at that meal by special invitation only.

In houses where there are young children old enough to dine at luncheon, ladies are oftener invited to luncheon than are gentlemen, unless the latter happen to be relatives or intimate friends; the reason for this being, that the bill of fare is a plain if a substantial one, and the presence of the children a restraint upon general conversation.

The most fashionable and usual hour for luncheon is two o'clock, but when children dine at that meal the hour is either one or half-past one.

The luncheon cover consists of two large knives and two large forks; a glass for sherry and one for claret. In most houses a *serviette* is included in the cover, while in others its use is dispensed with at this meal. For further description of the arrangements of the luncheon-table, *see* the "Management of Servants."

Those who are in the habit of frequently lunching out will have observed that, taking into consideration the variations offered by the seasons, the variety in the dishes given for luncheon is not great, and that the same dish, when in season, is constantly seen on most luncheon-tables. The circle of these dishes is a narrow one, perhaps because the choice of viands is more or less limited for luncheon, therefore those dishes are provided that are likely to suit the taste or palates of all, plain and light fare, easy of digestion, rather than rich made dishes being, as a rule, the order of things both in large and small establishments.

The generality of people do not care to eat highly-seasoned French dishes at this hour of the day, and greatly prefer a mutton cutlet, roast chicken or lamb. Those who give luncheons are aware of this predilection, and provide for their guests accordingly, giving only "those dishes that are sure to be eaten."

Inexperienced hostesses will find included in the following list the principal dishes usually given for luncheon in the most fashionable houses:—

"Mutton cutlets" is a standing dish and invariably given, whether a luncheon party consists of two or of ten people;

a man will eat a mutton cutlet when he declines every other dish, and ladies, as a rule, are also partial to a mutton cutlet, whether at luncheon or dinner. Cutlets are to the luncheon table what eggs and bacon are to the breakfast table, the dish *par excellence*.

The most popular ways of serving mutton cutlets for luncheon is plain, the sauce and vegetables being handed round separately, or with peas, stewed cucumber, spinach, or *à la Macédoine*, or with sauce *piquante*, or tomato sauce.

The cost of a dish of mutton cutlets for six people, served with sauce or vegetables, would amount to 4s., allowing 3 lbs. of the best end of neck of mutton, at 1s. per lb., and 1s. for either *petit pois*, cucumber, spinach, or sauce. Nine cutlets would make an average-sized dish for six people, and twelve cutlets for eight people.

Lamb cutlets are given, when lamb is in season, in preference to mutton, and they are either served plain or with asparagus, cucumber, or with *petit pois*. A dish of lamb cutlets for six people would cost from 3s. to 3s. 6d., allowing 3 lbs. of lamb, at 1s. 2d. per lb.; the vegetables or sauce served with the cutlets would cost 1s. or 1s. 6d., according to market price.

Veal cutlets are not a fashionable dish, and are seldom if ever given.

Chickens, either roast or boiled, rank next to cutlets amongst luncheon dishes, one good-sized chicken, at from 3s. 6d. to 3s. 9d. is usually provided.

Boiled chicken is as often given as is roast chicken, and is either served with celery sauce, or other white sauce, the cost of which sauce varies from 9d. to 1s.

Mayonnaise of chicken is a favourite luncheon dish, the cost of which for six people would amount to 5s. 8d., allowing 3s. for the chicken, ½ pint of cream at 1s., salad, 1s., and 4 eggs, 8d.

Roast pheasants, roast partridges, and roast hares are, in the game season, much given for luncheon, and the cost of these vary according to the market price; thus a pheasant would cost from 3s.

3d. to 4s. 6d.; partridges 4s. to 4s. 6d. the brace; a hare or leveret from 3s. 6d. to 4s. 6d.

For a party of six people one pheasant or one hare would be given, or three partridges, if partridges were given.

Roast lamb, either hot or cold, is much given for luncheon; the cost depending upon the season of the year and upon the market price, which varies from 1s. 6d. to 1s. per lb.; but joints of lamb, when lamb is at 1s. 6d. per lb., are not often provided for luncheon, at least in those houses where economy is studied.

Cold lamb is a favourite joint for luncheon, and is invariably accompanied by a salad. A fore-quarter of lamb is a choice cold joint, but a leg of lamb is, perhaps, more economical; the cost of either of these joints depends upon their weight. A fore-quarter of lamb would probably average 8 to 10 lbs., and being purchased by the quarter, might be had at 1s. 1d. per lb. in the summer months. A leg of lamb would average from 6 to 8 lbs., and would cost from 1s. to 1s. 6d. per lb., according to the time of year. In the early months of the year house-lamb cost from 1s. 4d. to 2s. per lb., say from February to April, while in June lamb is not dearer than mutton.

A hot roast loin of lamb is often given for luncheon, and averages about 6 lbs. in weight.

Roast or boiled mutton is generally provided when the luncheon is the children's dinner, although occasionally in the winter months a leg or loin of mutton is given where children do not dine at luncheon. The weight of a leg of mutton varies from 7 to 12 lbs., and costs from 10d. to 1s. per lb. The weight of a shoulder of mutton ranges from 5 to 10 lbs., at from 9d. to 11d. per lb. The same remark applies to a neck of mutton, which is another of the joints often chosen when children dine down at luncheon.

Hot roast beef is not usually selected for luncheon, save on Sundays, when it is a very general custom to have a large joint of beef on that day, weighing from 12 lbs. and upwards, either sirloin or ribs; the cost of which ranges from 10d. to 1s. 1d. per lb.

Cold roast beef is very frequently seen on the luncheon-table, not an uncut joint, but a large joint that has been cooked for dinner on, say, the previous evening.

Boiled beef, whether hot or cold, is not much in request at luncheon, unless it is glazed beef *à la mode*, which, on the contrary, is a popular cold luncheon dish; 6 lbs. of ribs of beef at 10d. per lb. would make a very fair-sized dish, allowing 1s. for herbs and spice, &c.

Fillet de boeuf is a dish often given for luncheon served with mushrooms, or *à la Macédoine*, or *à la Jardinière*; 2½ lbs. of rump-steak at 1s. 2d. per lb., and 1s. for vegetables or sauce ingredients, would make a luncheon dish for six people.

The same quantity of rump-steak broiled and served with either mushrooms or oyster-sauce, makes a more substantial than fashionable dish, except when a party of gentlemen are expected, when it is an appropriate luncheon dish to give. When served with oyster-sauce this dish would average 5s. 6d., allowing 2½ lbs. of steak at 1s. 2d. per lb., and a dozen and a half of oysters at 1s. 6d. per dozen, and 4d. for other ingredients; if cream were used the cost would be 1s. extra. When mushrooms are served with broiled steak the cost ranges from 9d. to 1s. 6d.

Rissoles made of beef, veal, chicken, ham, or game, are a very general luncheon dish, and not an expensive one, as the remains of the joints or birds from the dinner of the previous evening, usually furnish the materials of which they are composed, and the actual cost of these would not average more than 2s. for a dish of eight or ten rissoles.

Minced beef or minced veal, with poached eggs, are also tasty and economical luncheon dishes to give.

Hashed venison is much appreciated for luncheon; but this also is furnished from the haunch that has formed part of the dinner of the previous evening. From 2½ to 3 lbs. of venison would make a fair-sized dish for six people, cut in the thinnest of slices and served in the clearest of gravies.

Salmi of duck, or salmi of game, is a frequent luncheon dish. If not made from the poultry or game left from the dinner of the previous evening, a duck for the purpose would cost from 2s. 9d. to 3s., and 6d. or 9d. should also be allowed for sauce, with which it is served.

Patties are rarely given for luncheon, being considered more suitable for dinner.

Curry is an economical luncheon dish, and one that is rather liked by the generality of luncheon-eaters, and is made of either chicken, rabbit, or veal, but oftener of rabbit; the cost of a rabbit is from 1s. 3d. to 1s. 9d., and one rabbit would make a fair-sized dish of curry. Thus a rabbit at 1s. 9d. and curry-powder, stock, and rice at 8d., would bring the cost of this tasty dish to 2s. 5d.

Chicken curry is usually made from part of a chicken or chickens left from the dinner of the previous evening.

Quenelles of rabbit, chicken, or veal, are much fancied for luncheon, and this again is an inexpensive dish.

Fillets of rabbit, with sauce *à la Toulouse*, or with any *piquante* sauce, is also an inexpensive luncheon dish, the cost of which does not exceed 2s.

There are several appetizing ways of cooking a hare for luncheon besides roasting it, and a hare that has been much shot can only be dressed as an *entrée*, such as hare cutlets, or fillets of hare served with either a sweet or *piquante* sauce. A leveret at 3s. would make a good dish of cutlets or fillets for six people.

When this class of dish is provided it is as much approved of as one costing double its price, and a good housekeeper can give as tempting and smart-looking a luncheon by drawing upon the resources of her larder as can the more extravagant one, who, disdaining these aids, or ignorant of them, orders a fresh supply from poulterer or butcher wherewith to furnish her luncheon table.

Fish ranks last on this list of usual and favourite luncheon dishes by reason of its being hitherto seldom given, with a few exceptions, but there is now a decided partiality setting in for fish as a luncheon dish.

Cold salmon, garnished with cucumber, is a very popular dish. When it is served from a side-table 4 lbs. of salmon would be sufficient from which to help six people, but if the salmon were placed on the luncheon table to be helped by either host or hostess, a larger piece would be provided, weighing from 6 to 10 lbs.

The cost of salmon depends upon the time of year at which it is purchased; salmon in February is usually 4s. per lb.; in June it averages 1s. 6d. to 3s. per lb.

Salmon mayonnaise is also a favourite luncheon dish; 2 lbs. of salmon would make a dish for a luncheon party of eight people; 2 lbs., at 2s. 6d. per lb., which is the intermediate and general price of salmon from the 1st of May to the 31st of July, would cost 5s., to which must be added 1s. 6d. for salad, 1s. for ½ pint of cream, and 8d. for 4 eggs: thus a mayonnaise for a party of eight people would cost 9s. 2d.

Salmon is more or less an expensive dish for luncheon, but the above is au economical manner of dressing a small quantity of salmon left from the dinner of the previous evening.

Salmon souche is also sometimes given for luncheon, as are salmon cutlets.

Lobster salad is only given for luncheon by those who have a reputation for giving what are termed smart luncheons. The cost of a lobster salad for a party of six would amount to 6s. 8d., including a lobster, at 3s. 6d., salad, 1s. 6d., cream and eggs, 1s. 8d.

Dressed crab is rather liked for luncheon, and a crab may be purchased at from 2s. 6d. to 3s. 6d. ready dressed.

Hot dressed fish is sometimes given for luncheon, in which case it precedes the *entrée,* and is usually made of fish left from the previous evening's dinner, whether it be turbot, cod, or haddock.

Plover's eggs, with aspic jelly, is a fashionable but expensive dainty for luncheon. The cost of plover's eggs range from 3s. to 6s. per dozen. One dozen eggs would make a dish for a party of six, and the cost of sufficient aspic jelly to garnish the dish would not exceed 1s. 6d.

Collared eel is sometimes given for luncheon: the cost of this would average 3s. per dish. But this is not a popular dish with many, although enjoyed by the few. The same observation applies to cold eel pie. This also is liked by some and disliked by others. The cost of an eel pie is from 3s. to 4s.

Cold pigeon pie is sometimes given for luncheon, but more often in the country than in town. The cost of a pigeon pie containing 3 pigeons at 10d. each, if 1½ lbs. of steak at 1s. 2d. per lb., and 4 eggs, 1½d. each, with the ingredients for seasoning, and butter and flour for pastry, would amount to 5s. 8d.

The cost of a game pie, made with tongue, pheasants and truffles, would average from 15s. to 21s., while a smaller and plainer game pie would average from 8s. to 16s. according to size; and this also is oftener seen in country houses than in town houses.

Cold cutlets, with aspic jelly or *à la Macédoine,* are often given for luncheon in the summer months, and the cost of a dish for a party of six would average 4s.

Potatoes are always given at luncheon, either new potatoes, or mashed or fried potatoes, as the case may be. One other vegetable is also given, according to the season of the year, either cauliflower, Brussels sprouts, spinach or green peas, French beans or asparagus.

Soup is rarely given for luncheon, but as there are exceptions to every rule so there are some few houses in town where it is the practice to give it; clear soup, however, is the one given in preference to any other. For a party of six it would be necessary to provide 2 quarts of soup, and the cost of Julienne or Jardinière soup would average 1s. 9d. per quart if made at home, allowing 1½ lb. of shin of beef, at 7d. per lb., and 9d. for the necessary vegetables.

Although it is the custom to give not more than half-a-ladleful of soup to each person, yet the tureen should contain 2 quarts, or there would be too great a *rapprochement* between the ladle and the tureen, which in the ears of the guests would appear to be running things very close. For further information respecting soups and their various prices, see chapter on "Dinners."

The sweets given for luncheon usually consist of one hot and one cold; a hot pudding with a sweet sauce.

The following is the class of hot pudding usually given:—Brown bread pudding for a party of six people; the cost of this would amount to 3s. 9d., including cherries and cherry sauce.

A Cabinet-pudding, a Chestnut-pudding, a Ginger-pudding, a Lemon-pudding, &c., can also be made at the same cost, viz., 3s. 6d. to 4s., if made at home.

Sweet omelette and souffle are much given for luncheon; and a fair-sized omelette or souffle, sufficient for a party of six, can be made for 2s., if made with milk and not with cream; and it is not necessary to use cream for either of these sweets. Plum-pudding is given as a rule on Sunday, but it is otherwise seldom given for luncheon. The cost of a plum-pudding for a party of six would amount to 3s.

Apple fritters and orange fritters are occasionally given, and are an economical sweet. For a party of six a dozen fritters would be provided, and would cost not more than 1s. 6d.

Fruit tart generally finds favour with luncheon guests, and a tart for a party of six can be made at from 1s. 9d. to 2s. 6d., according to the fruit chosen.

When gooseberry or currant tart is given, cream is handed with it; ½ pint of cream would be sufficient, which raises the cost of these tarts to the extent of 1s.

Compotes of fruit are very popular as a luncheon sweet, whether made of apples, oranges, greengages, or peaches, &c. All compotes of fruit, with the exception of peaches and apricots, are very inexpensive thus a compote of oranges or apples for a party of six would cost 1s. 6d., and a compote of peaches twice that price, according to the season.

Normandy pippins covered with custard or whipped cream make a very good luncheon-sweet, and cost either 2s. 8d. or 3s., according to whether custard or cream is served with the apples.

With regard to different kinds of jellies given at luncheon, a *Macédoine* jelly ranks first, and is the most expensive. The cost of an ordinary-sized jelly of this description would average 4s. if made at home, and 7s. 6d. if ordered at a confectioner's; an orange jelly can be made at half the expense, viz., 2s., and would average 5s. at a confectioner's; a wine jelly without fruit would cost, made at home, 3s., if bought at a confectioner's, 7s. 6d.

Jelly left from the dinner of the previous evening is generally served in glasses, as half a mould can thus be made use of.

Iced gooseberry-fool is given when in season; sufficient for six or eight people would cost from 2s. 10d. to 3s.

Pastry is often given for luncheon, consisting of tartlets, cream-cakes, almond pastry, sponge-cake puddings, &c.; the cost of these made at home ranges from 1s. to 2s. 6d. per dozen, according to the class of materials used.

A luncheon cake is invariably given, the cost of which, if home-made, ranges from 1s. 6d. to 3s., according to the quality of the cake, whether plain plum or rich pound-cake. Between the cost of sweets made at home, and the cost of the same purchased at a confectioner's there is a very considerable difference; yet if a cook is not equal to making this class of sweet, it is more satisfactory to pay the confectioner's price, with the knowledge that the article will be up to the usual standard of an ordinary confectioner, than to attempt home-made dishes about which there is an uncertainty as to how they will turn out, or whether they will turn out at all. An inexperienced cook will waste almost as much as is required for any given dish in her unsuccessful essays; therefore in ordering a luncheon a mistress should always take into consideration the capabilities of her cook, and not be misled by her willingness to undertake anything and everything with the aid of a cookery-book, but should remember that experience has to be bought in addition to the cookery-book, and that the occasion of a luncheon-party is not the happiest moment at which to acquire it, the home circle being the legitimate field for first trials, with only the family to sit in judgment on the failure.

A young inexperienced mistress, whose cook is more confident than clever, is often led into making grave mistakes when ordering a luncheon or a dinner through her belief in the capabilities of her cook, who in her turn relies solely upon a recipe from a second or third class cookery-book, rather than upon practice which makes perfect. Thus, when a cook is not a skilful performer, and yet does certain things well, these things should be ordered for luncheon, however plain, in preference to more pretentious delicacies; and many of the sweets here mentioned, although generally given, are sufficiently simple to come within the scope of most cooks, and there are others equally simple that could be added to the list; but it is not considered necessary to enumerate them here, and the subjoined *menus* are given as an indication of the various styles of luncheon it is customary to give.

With regard to large luncheons, when the guests number from thirty to one hundred and upwards, and which partake of the character of a cold collation, the details and cost will be found at page 125.

Claret and sherry are the wines drunk at luncheon, claret being by far the most popular of the two; out of every six people four would most probably drink claret, while two only would drink sherry; therefore good claret is given for luncheon, and not light cup-claret. Claret at 60s. per dozen is given in some houses, while in others a less expensive, though fairly good claret, is given, at about 40s. per dozen. Again, in some houses sherry of the finest quality is drunk, while in others a lower price sherry is handed round. The quantity of wine drunk at luncheon is very small, and a party of six would not drink on an average more than 1½ bottles of claret and two-thirds of a bottle of sherry.

MENU OF LUNCHEON FOR SIX OR EIGHT PERSONS, JANUARY AND FEBRUARY

Dressed Fish

Mutton Cutlets   Tomato Sauce

Roast Pheasants

Vegetables

Mashed Potatoes   Spinach
Apricot Omelette   Compote of Apples
Pears   Grapes
Cake

MENU FOR SIX PERSONS, JANUARY AND FEBRUARY

Curry of Rabbit, with Rice

Roast Chicken

Vegetables

Mashed Potatoes   Cauliflower

Rhubarb Tart (hot)   Sponge Cream Cakes

Water Biscuits   Butter

Cake

MENU FOR EIGHT OR TEN PERSONS, MARCH AND APRIL

Soup Julienne

Lamb Cutlets with Cucumber
Roast Chickens

Vegetables

New Potatoes   Seakale

Plovers' Eggs in Aspic Jelly
Souffle   Maraschino Jelly
Biscuits   Butter
Cake

MENU FOR SIX PERSONS, MARCH AND APRIL

Fillet de Boeuf

Boiled Chicken, Celery Sauce

Vegetables

Potatoes   Cauliflowers

Lemon Pudding   Tartlets

Cake
Apples   Pears   Grapes

MENU FOR EIGHT PERSONS, MAY AND JUNE

Cold Salmon with Cucumber

Salmi of Quails

Vegetables

New Potatoes
Fore-quarter of Lamb (cold)

Green Peas
Salad

Brown Bread Pudding
Cake

Macédoine Jelly
Strawberries

MENU FOR EIGHT PERSONS, MAY AND JUNE

Mayonnaise of Salmon

Lamb Cutlets

Vegetables

New Potatoes

Peas

Roast Beef (cold)

Salad

Gooseberry Tart (hot)

Jelly

Cake

Strawberries

MENU FOR EIGHT OR TEN PERSONS, JULY AND AUGUST

Mayonnaise of Lobster

Hashed venison

Vegetables

Potatoes   French beans

Grouse   Cold lamb   Salad
Compote of Peaches   Ice Pudding
Cake   Fruit

MENU FOR SIX OR EIGHT PERSONS, JULY AND AUGUST

Mayonnaise of Chicken

Lamb Cutlets

Vegetables

Potatoes   Asparagus

Cold Pigeon Pie   Salad

Cherry Tart   Sponge Cake Pudding, with Preserves
Cake   Fruit

MENU FOR SIX OR EIGHT PERSONS, SEPTEMBER AND OCTOBER

Timbale of Chicken

Mutton Cutlets   Piquante Sauce

Roast partridges

Vegetables

Potatoes   French beans

Greengage Tart   Stewed Pears with Cream
Cake   Fruit

MENU FOR SIX OR EIGHT PERSONS, SEPTEMBER AND OCTOBER

Salmi of Duck

Broiled Steak with Mushrooms

Vegetables

Mashed Potatoes   Spinach

Roast Hare

Apple Charlotte   Compote of Fruit
Cake   Fruit

MENU FOR SIX OR EIGHT PERSONS, NOVEMBER AND DECEMBER

Mutton Cutlets à la Macédoine

Roast Wild Duck

Vegetables

Fried Potatoes   Brussels Sprouts

Cabinet Pudding   Almond Pastry

Water Biscuits   Butter   Stilton Cheese

MENU FOR EIGHT PERSONS, NOVEMBER AND DECEMBER

Quenelles of Rabbit

Leg of Welsh Mutton, Roast

Vegetables

Mashed Potatoes   Artichokes

Apple Fritters   Orange Jelly

Pears   Cake   Oranges

XI

DINNER PARTIES

Dinner Giving on various scales of Expense—Large Dinner Parties—Small Dinner Parties—Dinners regardless of expense—Dinners with due regard to expense—Fashionable Dishes—Popular Dishes—Useful Dishes—Dinner Wines—After Dinner Wines

THE SUBJECT OF DINNER GIVING is an interesting one to the many: to those who give large dinners, to those who give small dinners, and to diners-out in general. Every man considers himself more or less a judge of what constitutes a good dinner, and, doubtless, diners-out are thoroughly competent to form an opinion on this matter; but it is one thing to eat a dinner and to criticise or pronounce upon it afterwards, and another to arrange a *menu* that shall be perfect in its way, to find a cook whose co-operation throughout the whole may be thoroughly relied upon, and last, but not least, to bring such dinner within the individual means of each dinner giver. It is not everyone with wealth at command who understands the science of dinner giving. Again, it is not everyone with a talent in this direction whose pocket enables him to exercise it for the benefit of his friends, and the only resource left to one thus situated is to eat his friends' dinners, the while wishing that the said dinners had reached a higher standard of excellence.

Advice on the subject of dinner giving is rarely offered by one friend to another; such frankness or freedom of speech would most likely be considered in the light of an impertinence. People are very thin-skinned and rather touchy on the subject of the dinners they give to their friends, and therefore a guest, who is even an intimate friend of a host or hostess, would prefer to eat of a dozen bad dinners at his friend's table, from time to time, than to offer the faintest suggestions as to how those dinners might be improved, fearing, were he to do so, he would offend against the laws of good breeding observed between guest and host.

Forty years ago people were perhaps a trifle more blunt than in these days, and a story is told of a *bon vivant*, who when asked his opinion by his host of a dinner given in his honour, replied, "My dear fellow, sell your plate and get a cook." In illustration of this remark we may add that, the display of massive plate had been the great feature of the entertainment. *Apropos* of the story of long ago may be told one of to-day:—

An aesthetic lady had decorated her dinner-table with a profusion of beautiful flowers and had arranged the *menu* on the like ethereal principles. Her husband's satirical comment on the floral feast was *une autrefois, mon ami, moins de fleurs et plus de nourriture.*

The ostensible improvement in the dinners of today over those of a dozen years ago is that they are served more expeditiously, and that two in place of four *entrées* are given, and that dinner *à la Russe* is universal.

In two former works the subject of *diner à la Russe* and the method of serving dinner have been discussed in detail, it would therefore be superfluous to enter upon this branch of the subject in the present work.

The principal points to be considered in dinner giving are first, the arrangement of the *menu*, bearing in mind that each course should supplement the other, and that there should be no repetition but constant variety, and that the dishes of each course should offer a contrast, both in the materials employed and in the manner of cooking.

The time that should be occupied by the dinner is another important point, and the best of dinners should not be prolonged beyond an hour and a quarter. A saving of time is greatly facilitated by giving double *entrées* and double *entremets,* and by not crowding too many dishes into each course.

The average cost of all dishes suitable for dinners has been given in this chapter, and large and expensive dinners, or small and inexpensive dinners may be alike arranged for from the following tables, the newest and the most popular dishes being therein included.

The name of each dish has been given in French, by way of offering assistance when making out a *menu*, as not a few ladies find a difficulty in translating an English bill of fare into good French, while many of the sauces served with the various dishes, and the dishes themselves, cannot very well be rendered into English. Some ladies make laughable mistakes when writing out a *menu* in French, thus *saut rôti* appeared for roast goose on a fashionable *menu* not long ago, to the no little amusement of the guests.

Soup is perhaps the least expensive item in the cost of a dinner-party, but as it comes first on the *menu* it is naturally the first point to be considered, and soup is to those who understand dining and dinner giving—as it should be understood—the key note of a dinner, and by the class and quality of the soup given a very fair estimate is arrived at as to the style of dinner which is likely to follow.

Soup making is perhaps as good a test as any that can be applied to discover the capabilities of a cook, and although considered to be the simplest and lightest portion of her labours, yet experience, intelligence, judgment and attention are required on the part of a cook to produce a delicately-flavoured high-class soup. Many people entertain an idea that soup interferes with digestion, and that although they commence dinner with it as a matter of course, because it is the fashion to do so, they would be better without it. But Sir Henry Thompson, in his interesting little work on "Food and Feeding," says, "that there appears to be no foundation for this belief, and that a clear soup, or the fluid constituents of a *purée,* disappear almost immediately after entering the stomach, being absorbed by the proper vessels, and in no way interfere with the gastric juice, which is stored in its appropriate cells ready for action. The habit of commencing dinner with soup has without doubt its origin in the fact that aliment in this fluid form—in fact, ready digested—soon enters the blood and rapidly refreshes the hungry man, who after a considerable fast and much activity, sits down with a sense of exhaustion to commence his principal meal. In two or three minutes after taking a plate of good warm *consommé* the feeling of exhaustion disappears. Soup introduces at once into the system a small instalment of ready-digested food, and saves the short period of time which must be spent by the stomach in deriving some portion of nutriment from solid aliment, as well as indirectly strengthening the organ of digestion itself for its forthcoming duties."

Soup made by the indifferent cook, whether concocted in the home kitchen, or the hotel kitchen, or the confectioner's kitchen, often falls far short of the ideal soup.

Soup of a dark mahogany brown, the result of high colouring, attained by the free use of Yorkshire Relish, Worcestershire Sauce, or burnt sugar, and not in any way due to the strength of the stock employed, with particles of fat floating here and there on the surface, and atoms of a stringy substance doing duty for vegetables, are too often presented under the title of clear soup, Julienne, Jardinière, or Printanière, and the like, whereas the genuine article, the real thing, the *consommé claire* is, when made by a good cook, of a light golden shade, with a delicate aroma of fresh vegetables about it, brightly clear and free from every scintillation of fat.

The substantial soups, again, commonly called thick soups by these not over-learned in the manner of making them, more than justify the appellation of thick, as arrowroot and flour enter largely into their composition, while, for flavour, they depend upon indifferent sherry and the heterogeneous contents of the spice-box; the forcemeat balls, and hard pieces of gristle which abound in this gluey mixture do not assist to render it more palatable.

The soups given at dinner-parties vary in a measure according to the season of the year, each season offering a certain amount of variety and choice, although in reality all soups may be said to come under two heads, the clear soups under that of *consommé,* and the thick soups under that of *purée.*

Amongst what may be considered favourite soups, or soups most generally given, are the following:—

Consommé à la d'Escitignac, Printanière, Jardinière, Consommé au Vermicelle claire, Ox Tail Soup, Soup Brunoise, Consommé à l'Impériale, Consommé au Riz à l'Italienne, Soup Crécy, Consommé au Macaroni, Purée de Volaille à la Reine, Purée de Gibier, Mock Turtle, Mulligatawny, Hare Soup, Bonne Femme, Palestine Soup, Oyster Soup, Bisque d'Ecrevisses, Purée de Pois St. Germain, Giblet Soup, Purée de Pois Verts, Consommé de Céleri, Clear Turtle, Thick Turtle.

The cost of the various soups here mentioned average if bought at a confectioner's from 4s. to 6s. per quart, when made at home a far superior soup is produced at from 1s. to 1s. 6d. per quart, according to the class of soup required. Soups made from stock are less expensive than those made from game, calf's head, &c.

The cost of either Oyster Soup or Bisque d'Ecrevisse would average 2s. 6d. per quart.

Two descriptions of soup are always given at large dinner-parties, one *consomm*é and one *purée.*

Clear turtle or Tortue Claire is very much given at both small and large dinners by those who are inclined to pay the price for it, namely, one guinea per quart; but both Tortue Claire and Tortue Liée are both given at men's dinners when the arrangements are on a grand scale.

For a dinner of eight people, one quart of turtle would be the quantity to order in addition to a second soup.

Although it is usual to give two kinds of soup for a large dinner party, a clear or thick soup and a white soup, yet it is necessary to provide a larger quantity of the one than of the other; white soup is but little fancied by dinner guests in consequence, perhaps, of cream entering largely into its composition, and rich soups of this nature are supposed to be a trying beginning for the courses to follow.

With regard to the quantities required for a dinner party, it must be borne in mind that the proportions differ from that by which other entertainments are regulated; that is to say, such as providing for two-thirds, one-half, or even one-third of the guests of given dishes; in the case of dishes that form the courses of a dinner, it is necessary to allow sufficient of each dish for over and above the full number of guests present. A dinner, unlike a ball-supper, is the principal meal of the day, and the choice of each dish must be allowed to all, and the acceptance of the same provided for; but there is a little elasticity in this rule as regards soup, especially in the case of turtle soup, a soup to which ladies are not particularly partial; again, as regards white soups, it would be sufficient to provide for two-thirds of the guests present; all other soups are provided in accordance with the full number of guests present, the proportion being 1 pint to every three persons, and 1 pint for waste for instance, for a dinner party of eighteen, 7 pints of clear soup and 5 pints of white soup would be the proportion.

For the manner of serving soup, as well as the various courses of a dinner, see Chapter, Waiting at Dinner, in the work entitled "The Management of Servants."

A choice of soups, represented by two soups, is often given at small dinners also, and when the giver of the feast is a *bon vivant* this is invariably done; but at the usual run of small dinners of from six to eight persons, it is considered sufficient to give but one soup, this would be selected from the clear soups before-mentioned, or from the *purées* of game, or brown soups in general.

At large dinner parties two kinds of fish are always given, and even at small dinner parties of from eight to ten it is rather the custom to give two kinds of fish; some people, again, consider that choice in the fish course is not necessary, and, therefore, they allow of no choice, beyond endeavouring to provide what they consider a choice piece of salmon or turbot, but these people do not profess to be smart dinner givers, yet often succeed in giving really excellent dinners through not extending the *menu* beyond the powers of the cook.

Others, again, are desirous of cutting down the expenses in the arrangements for a dinner party, and after all, when a choice is provided, a guest never eats but of one fish, with the exception of whitebait. When two sorts of fish are given, it is needless to say that they would be dressed in different ways, boiled and fried or broiled, and that a large and a smaller kind of fish would be chosen, such as salmon and smelts, turbot and whiting, &c.

In providing fish for a dinner party, the proportion would be to allow of each fish for two-thirds of the guests present.

Oysters when given do not form part of the fish course, but precede the soup. Half-a-dozen oysters would be the proportion to provide for each guest. A plate containing six oysters is placed before each guest, lemon, pepper, vinegar, and brown bread and butter are handed after the guests are seated at table. The cost of oysters averages 3s. per dozen.

Salmon ranks first in the fish course at all dinner parties, and very justly so, as it is certainly the king amongst fish, not only for its delicious flavour, but also for its nutritive qualities, half a pound of fresh salmon being almost equal in nutritive value to the same weight of fresh meat. Salmon, on account of its price, is confined principally to the tables of the rich, but occasionally it comes within reach of those possessing very moderate means. Formerly so plentiful was it in our rivers, that we are told it was made a condition in the indentures of apprentices that they should not be fed upon it more than a certain number of days in the week—truly, in those days it was the food of the poor, whereas now it is but the luxury of the rich.

Crimped salmon is greatly preferred by connoisseurs to uncrimped salmon, but a high price is charged by the fishmonger for salmon that has undergone this process, as it possesses a far more delicate flavour, but this delicate flavour rapidly disappears, and crimped salmon cannot be kept as long as salmon that has not been crimped.. Salmon is crimped immediately after it is caught, and before the *rigor mortis* has set in; there is then a fluid of a gelatinous creamy nature lying between the muscles, the flesh is easily divided, and presents a curdy appearance, and not only is the flavour enhanced, but it is considered more digestible when so prepared; kind-hearted women shudder at the idea of thus inflicting deep cuts upon fish that is yet alive, and consider it a case for the intervention of the Secretary of the Society for the Prevention of Cruelty to Animals, if fish comes under their jurisdiction.

Salmon is served either in slices crimped, or in the piece of so many pounds in weight, according to the size of the dinner party, and it is usual to allow 6 lbs. for a party of eight if only one fish were given, or 10 lbs. for a party of eighteen, as two kinds of fish would be given.

The price of salmon ranges from 2s. 6d. to 4s. 6d. per lb., but the average price of crimped salmon is 3s. 6d. per lb. In the months of July and August salmon is sold sometimes at from 1s. 3d. to 2s. per lb., but when it has arrived at this price it is no longer esteemed a luxury.

Salmon is occasionally served as an *entrée*, such as salmon quenelles, or salmon boudin, &c.; water souchet of salmon is also given in turn with grilled salmon; but the quantity of salmon required for a given number would average the same as if simply boiled and served with any of the sauces here given.

The sauces given with salmon are Ravigote, Cardinale, Hollandaise, Tartare, Fennel, Génoese, Caper, and Lobster; of these sauces Ravigote and Tartare seem to be the most popular, and Lobster the least so. The cost of either would average 1s. per pint, with the exception of lobster sauce, the expense of which would be from 2s. to 2s. 6d. per pint.

Cucumber is always served, or handed, with salmon, in addition to the fish sauce selected.

Cod and turbot follow next in the order of dinner fish; crimped cod is always preferred to uncrimped cod, and, as in the case of salmon, a higher price is charged for it in consequence. The price of cod and turbot ranges from 10d. to 1s. 6d. per lb.; the various sauces eaten with cod and turbot will be found in the list of fish sauces here appended. Cod is usually dressed plain, but occasionally *au gratin*; turbot is also dressed plain, and occasionally *en filets*. The quantity of either cod or turbot required for a dinner party of a given number would average the same as salmon.

The sauces with which cod is served are:—

Oyster Sauce, Sauce à l'Hollandaise, and Sauce à la Maître

d'Hôtel. Of these oyster sauce is the most expensive, and would probably average 2s. 6d. per pint, whilst the cost of the others would be 1s. per pint.

The sauces eaten with turbot are Sauce à l'Hollandaise, Sauce Ravigote, Sauce Cardinale, Sauce à la Parisienne, Sauce à la Normande, Sauce à l'Indienne, and Lobster Sauce.

The cost of these sauces averages 1s. per pint, with the exception of lobster sauce, which would amount to 2s. 6d. per pint.

Soles form a second dinner fish, and as such are very generally given, served *en filets*, with a variety of sauces, or dressed plain.

The sauces served with sole include Sauces Cardinale, Hollandaise, Maître d'Hôtel, Colbert, Tartare, &c. &c.

The price of soles varies according to size from 2s. to 7s. per pair, and the number of fillets also depends upon the size of the sole.

In providing fillets of soles for a given number of guests, one fillet would be the proportion to allow to each person if another fish were given in addition to soles, otherwise the quantity of fillets required would be increased by one of the whole.

Mackerel and whiting are also favourite fish for dinner in addition to the larger fish.

The sauce usually served with mackerel are fennel, maître d'hotel, and ravigote.

Whiting is served with the same sauces with the exception of fennel.

The number of mackerel required for a given number of guests depends upon the size of the fish; the proportion would probably be one mackerel to three persons. The cost of mackerel ranges from 4d. to 8d. each, according to the season. The sauce would average 1s. per pint.

The proportion of whiting would be one whiting to each person. The cost of whiting is from 3s. to 4s. per dozen.

Mackerel is served either boiled, grilled, or *en filets*, while whiting are generally fried.

Dublin Bay haddocks and fresh herrings are also given when first in season but again, by way of variety, in the fish course, haddocks are served with oyster sauce and sauce Hollandaise; and herrings with mustard sauce.

The price of haddocks varies from 1s. 4d. to 2s., according to size. The price of fresh herrings averages 2s. per dozen. In providing haddocks the proportion would be one haddock to four persons, and of fresh herrings, one herring to each person; but with all fish provided by the dozen, it is always understood that a margin is necessary over and above the number of guests.

Smelts and red mullet are much given when in season, red mullets are served with a piquante sauce, smelts are served with sauce Tartare, sauce Hollandaise, or melted butter. The proportion of smelts would be from two to four to each person, according to the size of the smelts.

Whitebait is always esteemed a delicacy, especially when first in season, but it greatly depends upon the care bestowed upon cooking it whether it is or not the *bonne bouche* that *bon vivants* consider it. So interesting is the subject to some dinner givers, that they deign to acquaint themselves with this branch of cookery if with no other, and a host will converse at length as to the exact moment when the basket should be dropped into the boiling lard, and as to how many moments it should remain there. Whitebait is quite independent of sauce, and a squeeze of lemon handed when it is served, together with a slice of thin brown bread and butter is all that is required to give a zest to the enjoyment of this much lauded dish.

In providing whitebait for a dinner party, the proportion would be one pint to every three persons. The cost of whitebait is from 1s. to 2s. per pint, according to season.

When eels are given at a dinner-party, which is but seldom, they are either served as a water *souchet*, or are stewed or spitchcocked; but eels as a rule are principally confined to the family dinner-table when the head of the family has a *penchant* for them, as they are far from being every one's taste.

The price of eels is from 10d. to 1s. 4d. per lb., and the proportion would be 1 lb. to every three persons.

John Dory and sturgeon are also but seldom given, and are

oftener seen at family dinners than at dinner-parties. Skate and gurnet are also fish answering this description, and which are given for economical reasons at a family dinner. The cheaper kinds of fish are not given at dinner-parties for the simple reason that the laws of hospitality call upon a host to give the best of its kind to his friends, and as the better kinds of fish offer at all seasons of the year ample variety from which to choose when ordering a dinner, it would be rather going out of the way were the meaner kinds of fish to be selected, simply to prove what may be done with common materials, with the aid of uncommon skill; but as a triumph of cookery combined with economy these supplies may be drawn upon once in a way to every one's satisfaction, although the rule of life is not to pass by the prime and the best to take the inferior and the worst when the former is within reach; it would be only an eccentricity of will that would govern the act rather than actual preference.

Again, as regards fresh water fish—pike, carp, perch, roach, dace, &c., an amateur sportsman keenly enjoys the spoil of his own rod, and is never so happy as when he can induce others to join him at his own dinner-table, or to accept a basket of fish for their own dinner-tables. A trout fresh from the stream, a baked pike well stuffed, are tasty things in their way, but no little part of the enjoyment of such fish lies in the fact that they are caught in some well-known stream or river by the rod of a friend, if not by one's own rod, and are the result of both patience and skill; while if supplied by a fishmonger, they would be judged upon their own merits only, and probably be pronounced insipid and flavourless, and hardly worth purchasing. Hence it follows that fresh water fish rarely appear in the fish course at a dinner-party, save as evidence of the hosts' skill as an angler, and to afford him an opportunity of relating his exploits in landing a fine pike weighing some 32 lbs., whilst inviting them to eat one of the same finny tribe weighing not more than 6 lbs.—a pike over this weight is considered coarse and uneatable.

Trout and tench, however, are an exception to the rule, which applies to fresh water fish in general, and are considered very good eating. Thames trout, for instance, being highly estimated, and are in season during May, June, and July. The cost of a Thames trout is equal to that of a salmon trout, and is eaten with the same sauce as is salmon. Tench is served with Dutch sauce, and is occasionally given at dinner-parties in addition to other fish.

It is no longer the fashion to give four *entrées*; the number has been reduced to three at large dinner-parties, and to two at small dinner-parties. Formerly the *entrées* were of a most substantial character, and invariably comprised cutlets, patties, and *filet de boeuf*; now the idea is to give *entrées* of the highest possible character to tempt the appetite rather than to satisfy it, and the *entrées* here enumerated include those most generally given both at small and unpretentious dinners, and at large and expensive dinners. Some dinner givers have revived the old custom—that of serving the removes before the *entrées*, but to the majority of diners out this revival does not commend itself. Unless the joint is a very choice one, a haunch of venison, for instance, the *relevé*, or remove, is an every-day affair, while the art, the skill, the science, the triumph, of cookery, are revealed in the made dishes, viz., the *entrées*. Again, it is only those who have a well-established reputation for giving good dinners who can successfully attempt innovations of any kind without running the risk of being considered worse than eccentric—ignorant of how a dinner should be served, and of having their dinners pronounced odd and extraordinary. Thus it is that the generality of mankind follow in the beaten track, and leave it to more daring spirits to be the pioneers of any new custom or fashion in the art of dinner giving.

When mutton cutlets are given, they are served with the following sauces or manner of serving:—

Côtelettes à la Reforme, Côtelettes à la Soubise, Côtelettes à la Russe, Côtelettes à la Bretonne, Côtelettes à la Maintenon, Côtelettes with Sauce Piquante, Côtelettes with Tomato sauce or all Tomato, Côtelettes à la Macédoine, mutton cutlets with spinach; Côtelettes à l'Indienne, Côtelettes à la Provençale.

Lamb cutlets or Côtelettes d'Agneau as they appear in French cookery-books and on French *menus*, are served either with cucumber (Concombre), with peas (Aux Petits Pois), with asparagus (Pointes d'Asperges) or à la Duchesse, à la Princesse, à la Lucullus.

In providing cutlets for a dinner-party, it is usual to allow one cutlet to each person, with a margin of from four to six cutlets.

In computing the cost of either lamb or mutton-cutlets, the average is to allow four lamb-cutlets to the pound, and three mutton-cutlets to the pound; thus, for a party of twelve, from 4 to 5 lbs. of lamb and 6 lbs. of mutton would be required for cutlets.

Pork-cutlets, with sauce Robert, are occasionally given at dinner-parties; but they are not by any means considered a fashionable *entrée*. Veal-cutlets are regarded in the same light by dinner-givers, and are, therefore, avoided as being too heavy and indigestible to be included amongst *entrées*.

Partridge-cutlets are, when given, a very popular *entrée*; for a party of twelve people, from three to four brace of partridges would be required. Thus, these cutlets would amount to 18s. or 19s.

Sweetbreads appear to have taken their stand as a ubiquitous *entrée,* and few *menus* are arranged without including them.

The sweetbread of the calf is the most delicate in flavour; but it not unfrequently happens that lamb sweetbreads are supplied in place of those of the calf, and the latter are not nearly so good as are the former.

Probably, the high price charged for this much-esteemed delicacy, which is but the pancreas gland of the animal, is an additional reason for its being so great a favourite with dinner-givers, apart from its digestive qualities and its suitability for the position it occupies in the ranks of *entrées*.

Amongst the favourite modes of serving sweetbreads (Ris de Veau), are the following:—

Sweetbreads à la Financière, Ris de Veau à la St. Cloud, Ris de Veau à la Monarque, Ris de Veau Piqué aux Epinards, Ris de Veau à la Toulouse, Escalopes de Ris de Veau, Croquettes of Sweetbreads, Sweetbreads with Mushrooms, Ris de Veau à la

Jardinière, Krömeskys of Sweetbreads, Sweetbreads à la Villeroi, Darioles de Ris de Veau.

The price of sweetbreads varies from 6s. to 12s. per couple; in providing sweetbreads for a dinner-party, the proportion would be two sweetbreads to every three persons.

The cost of serving sweetbreads with either of the sauces, vegetables, &c., here mentioned, would average 3s. per dish, in addition to the cost of the sweetbreads.

With some dinner-givers, Patties, Quenelles, and Croustades, rank higher than the preceding *entrées*; and are, therefore, oftener given.

Amongst the patties most given are, Petits Pâtés de Homard, Pâtés de Moelle, Pâtés d'Ortolans, Pâtés de Volaille, Petits Pâtés à la Financière, Petits Pâtés de Crevettes, Oyster Patties, Pâtés à la Reine, Petit Pâté de Foie Gras, Vol au Vent à la Financière, Vol au Vent de Volaille, Vol au Vent de Mauviettes.

The cost of making any of the Pâtés here mentioned, for a party of eighteen, would average 8s., or for a party of twelve, 6s.

The cost of any of the Vol au Vents here mentioned, would average 8s. each; and for a party of eighteen, two Vol au Vents would be required. Vol au Vents of chicken average 6s. each.

Croustades of the following order are very generally given:—

Croustade de Moelle, Croustade de Mauviettes, Croustade de Cailles, Croustade de Foies Gras aux Truffes, Petites Croustades de Laitances. These are usually made from the soft roe of mackerel or herring, and are a *bonne bouche* to epicures.

The cost of making croustades of larks, Mauviettes, for a party of eighteen would amount to from 7s. to 8s.; and of quails, from 8s. to 10s. Croustade de Foie Gras would average the same. Croustade de Moelle would average 4s., and Petites Croustades de Laitances about the same.

The following Quenelles are much appreciated:—

Quenelles de Poulets aux Truffes, Quenelles de Poulets à la Maréchale, Quenelles de Volaille à 1'Estragon, Quenelles of Pheasants, Quenelles of Partridge, Quenelles of Grouse, Quenelles de Veau aux Petits Pois, Quenelles of Hare, Quenelles of Rabbit.

The cost of providing quenelles of chicken, pheasant, or hare, for a party of eighteen, would average 9s., allowing for a double *entrée*; a single *entrée* for nine people would average 6s. Quenelles of partridge or grouse would average 13s. for a party of eighteen, allowing for a double *entrée*, or 10s. for a party of twelve. Quenelles of veal and quenelles of rabbit are very inexpensive *entrées*; and a double *entrée* for eighteen people would not cost more than from 5s. to 6s.

Amongst the fillets given are the following:—

Filets de Canetons, Filets de Poulet aux Truffes, Filet de Volaille, Filet de Perdreaux, Filets of Grouse, Filets of Wild-duck, Filets of Teal, Filets de Lièvre, Filets de Lapereaux Piqués à la Toulouse, Filets de Pigeons aux Champignons, Filets de Tête de Veau, Filets de Homard.

In providing this description of *entrée,* the cost would depend upon the birds selected, fillets of partridges and grouse running more expensive than fillets made from poultry, wild-fowl, or ground-game; for a party of eighteen, a double *entrée* of fillets would be required, which would average 10s. per dish, allowing two brace of partridges or two brace of grouse to the dish.

Fillets of spring-ducklings would average the same price, putting the ducklings at from 3s. to 4s. each.

Fillets made from fuller-grown birds, when the season is more advanced, would not average more than 6s. per dish, or 12s. for a double *entrée.*

Fillets of wild-duck, chicken, pigeon, and hare, would average for this number of guests 5s. 6d. per dish, or 11s. for a double *entrée.*

For a party of twelve, the cost would be reduced by one-fourth; and for a party of fifteen, by one-sixth.

The cost of Filet de Tête de Veau for a party of eighteen, would average 7s.

Entrées of venison principally consist of hashed venison with clear gravy, haricot of venison, cutlets of venison, fillets of venison.

Amongst favourite *entrées* are the following:—

Salmi de Perdreaux à la Provençale, Salmi de Perdreaux aux Champignons, Salmi de Perdreaux à la Financière, Salmi de

Bécasses à la Chasseur or à la Bonne-bouche, Salmi de Cailles aux Truffes, Salmi of Grouse, Coquilles à la Périgord, Krômeskys de Foies Gras, Salmi of Wild Duck, Salmi de Faisan à la Financière, Salmi de Faisan à la Richelieu, Boudin de Perdreaux à la Printanière, Wood-cocks à la Périgord, Ortolans à la Provençale, Mauviettes à la Lucullus, Boudin de Mauviettes, Turban de Mauviettes, Croquettes of Oysters, Krömeskys d'huîtres, Krômeskys de Boeuf, Turban de Cailles à la Toulouse, Petits Timbales de Macaroni aux Bécassines, Petit Timbale de Volaille à la Mazarin, Timbale of Macaroni, Escalopes de Volaille à la Lucullus, Pain de Volaille aux Truffes, Boudins de Volaille à la Lucullus, Poulet à la Marengo, Fricassée de Poulets, Bouchées à la Reine, Bouchées à la Pompadour, Boudins de Volaille, Suprêmes de Volaille à l'écarlate, Krômeskys à la Russe, Croquettes de Volaille aux Champignons, Rissoles de Volaille, Curry de Volaille à l'Indienne, Casserolle à la Rome, Marinade de Volaille, Suprême de Volaille à la Macédoine, Blanquette de Volaille aux Concombres, Poulet à la Tartare, Croquettes de Foies Gras, Chartreuse de Volaille, Grilled Chicken with Mushrooms, Boudin de Lapereaux à la Reine, Boudin de Faisan à la Richelieu, Chartreuse de Perdreaux, Suprême de Faisan, Purée de Marrons, Compote de Pigeons aux Pois, Salmi of Pigeon, Boudin of Grouse.

The cost of making my of the above *entrées* for a party of eighteen would average from 10s. to 14s., allowing for a double *entrée*.

The following inexpensive *entrées* can be made at home for a party of eighteen at from 7s. to 8s., allowing for a double *entrée*.

Escalopes de Foies Gras; Rissoles de Gibier; Grenadines de Boeuf aux Tomates; Beef Olives à l'Espagnol; Fricandeau de Veau; Grenadines de Veau aux Epinards; Rissoles de Veau; Croquettes de Veau; Tendons de Veau aux Pois Verts; Veal Olives; Curry of Rabbit à l'Indienne; Turban of Rabbit à la Financière.

It is now the fashion with some dinner-givers to include a *chaudfroid* in the course of *entrées*, that is in place of giving three hot *entrées*, two *entrées* and one *chaudfroid* would be given, and even at small dinner parties, one *entrée* and one *chaudfroid* is sometimes given in place of two *entrées*; but unless everything is very well done throughout the whole of the dinner, it would be considered pretentious to attempt anything so fashionable as a *chaudfroid*.

The price of a *chaudfroid* averages that of an *entrée* of the same class; the proportion required is also identical.

The following are considered favourite *chaudfroids* amongst the *élite* of dinner-givers.

Jambon Glacé aux Epinards; Chaudfroid de Cailles à la Lucullus; Chaudfroid de Bécassines en Caises; Souffles de Homard Glacés; Chaudfroid de Perdreaux; Galantine de Cailles à la Périgord; Tomates Farcies; Oeufs de Pluviers en Aspic.

Of all the *relevés*, or removes, here mentioned a *hanche* of venison is the most expensive, its price being £2 2s.; but as half a buck can be purchased for the same price, those who are in the habit of giving venison order half a buck in preference to a haunch only. Venison ranks high amongst *relevés* in general estimation, and when given it does not require the support of a second *relevé*. Doe venison is considered very inferior to buck venison, and is, therefore, seldom given by good judges.

A neck of venison is liked by many, and is frequently given; but it is not so esteemed as is a haunch, and, therefore, it does not stand alone amongst *relevés*, but is given in conjunction with poultry.

With regard to mutton, four-year-old mutton is now a thing of the past. Formerly people could not dine unless the saddle of mutton was cut from a four-year-old sheep, now the mutton sent to table is from eighteen months to two years old, and the younger generation are not sure that it is not preferable to the much prized four-year-old mutton. The saddle is still considered the prime joint to give, and the average weight is from 14 to 16 lbs., and the average price 11d. to 1s. per lb.

A well hung leg or loin of mutton is often given at small dinner parties, although less frequently than is a saddle. At small dinner parties one *relevé* only would be given, which would consist of a joint. At larger dinner parties, starting from twelve in number, two *relevés* would be given, one of meat and one of poultry. At banquet-dinners, or dinners given on a very large and expensive scale, three *relevés* are occasionally provided; but this is an exception to the rule in dinner-giving.

A sirloin of beef is considered more appropriate for a family dinner than for a dinner party, and when beef is given, *Filet de Boeuf* is chosen in preference to a sirloin of beef. *Filet de Boeuf* was formerly included amongst the *entrées*, but it has now taken its proper place amongst the more substantial *relevés*.

If *Filet de Boeuf* were given, from 8 to 10 lbs. would be provided for a party of eighteen; and if sirloin were selected, the weight would be about 14 lbs. The price of beef ranges from 1s. to 1s. 2d. per lb., according to whether it is fillet or rump-steak.

Fillet of veal is even more seldom given than is sirloin of beef. 10 lbs. would be a fair-sized fillet to give; the price of which ranges from 10d. to 1s. per lb.

Lamb is much given at dinner parties in the summer months. A fore-quarter of lamb is the joint usually selected, the weight of which runs about 12 lbs., at from 11d. to 1s. 4d. per lb., according to the season.

Hot ham, with broad beans as a *relevé*, is considered rather a dainty dish to provide, especially at men's dinners, and when broad beans are not in season, salad or spinach take their place.

When two *relevés* are given, the second *relevé* generally consists of poultry. The cost of a capon, or *poularde*, ranges from 8s. to 12s., according to size, to which about 3s. must be added for ingredients with which to serve.

The price of a fine pair of chickens for roasting would average from 8s. to 9s. Either tongue or ham accompanies roast or boiled chickens; the cost of the former would amount to from 4s. to 6s. When a ham is given as a *relevé* one weighing 16 lbs. would be provided, ranging from 1s. to 1s. 3d. per lb.

If a fine turkey were provided, it would probably weigh from 14 to 16 lbs., or if a hen turkey, the weight would probably be from 8 to 10 lbs.; the average price of turkey is 1s. per lb.

The following are the *relevés* is most chiefly given:—

Hanche de Venaison Rôtie; Hanche de Mouton; Selle de

Mouton Rôtie; Gigot de Mouton à la Provençale; Gigot d'Agneau Rôti; Sirloin of Beef Roast; Rond de Veau Rôti à la Jardinière; Filet de Boeuf Piqué; Filet de Boeuf à la Jardinière; Filet de Boeuf Grillé Maître d'Hôtel; Tête de Veau à la Tortue; Quartier d'Agneau Rôti; Selle d'Agneau; Poulets à l'Ivorie; Jambon de Yorc et Fêves de Marais; Jambon de Yorc et Salade Française; Poulet et Langue à la Jardinière ou à la Macédoine; Chapon Bouilli; Purée de Céleris; Poulardes truffées à la Périgord; Chapons truffés à la Périgord; Dinde Rôti; Dinde Boulli.

The second service is commenced with *rôts*. At large dinner parties two *rôts* are given; at small dinner parties but one *rôt* is given. In providing two *rôts* the proportion would be to allow for two-thirds of each *rôt*. Thus for a party of eighteen, a brace of fine pheasants and 1 dozen snipes would be given, or a couple of ducklings and 1 dozen quails, and so on. When only one *rôt* is given, the rule is to provide for the entire number of guests. Thus for a dinner party of from eight to nine guests, a turkey poult, or two brace of woodcocks, or one brace of pheasants, &c., would be given.

The price of game, poultry, and birds fluctuates according to the season of the year, but the following prices appended to the *rôts* here given are a very general average, and these *rôts* are considered the most choice in their various seasons:—

Ducklings, 6s. to 12s. per couple; green goslings, 6s. to 9s. each; guinea-fowl, 4s. 6d. to 5s. each. Capons are much preferred to guinea-fowls, as the latter are considered to have a strong flavour. The price of capons is from 7s. 6d. to 13s.; pea-fowl, from 10s. to 16s. each. The price of turkey poults, 7s. 6d. to 11s. 6d.; these are reckoned excellent as a second-course *rôt*. Spring chickens range from 8s. to 9s. per couple; quails, from 10d. to 1s. 6d. each; golden plovers and teal, from 1s. to 1s. 3d. each; widgeon, 1s. 3d. to 1s. 9d. each; wild ducks, from 7s. to 8s. per couple; partridges, 4s. 6d. a brace; pheasants, from 7s. to 9s. a brace; grouse, 6s. to 8s. a brace; black game, about the same; larks, from 2s. 6d. to 3s. 6d. per dozen; pigeons, from 9d. to 1s. each; Bordeaux, do., 1s. to 1s. 9d.;

woodcocks, 3s. 6d. to 4s. 6d. each; snipes, 1s. 3d. to 1s. 9d. each; ortolans, 2s. 6d. to 4s. 6d. each; leverets, in May and June, from 4s. to 8s. each.

Canetons aux Cressons; Green Gosling; Guinea-fowl; Pea-fowl; Capons, Petits Poulets, et Langue à la Printanière; Dindonneaux; Pluviers; Sarcells; Perdreaux; Grouse; Black Game; Faisans; Mauviettes; Widgeon; Buffs and Reeves, Pigeons; Bordeaux Pigeons; Canards sauvages; Cailles bardées; Ortolans bardées; Bécasses; Bécassines; Levraut.

The vegetables given at a dinner party form quite a feature in themselves, and no little judgment is required in their selection, that each vegetable may thoroughly harmonize with the course in which they are included.

Potatoes are not eaten in the fish course, save when new potatoes are given with salmon, or when dressed fish is served with mashed potatoes; neither are vegetables handed with the *entrées*.

Two plain vegetables and salad are always given with the *relevés* or removes in the first course, and one or two dressed vegetables are given with the *rôts* in the second course, and very often a dressed vegetable is included in the savory *entremets*, in which case only one dressed vegetable would be given with the *rôts*. *Pommes de terre frites* generally accompany the *rôts*, with or without a second dressed vegetable, especially in the game season, when vegetables do not offer so great a choice.

The price of vegetables depends upon whether they are forced vegetables of the winter or early spring months, or merely those in season.

In providing vegetables for a party of eighteen the cost would average 18s. allowing for two dressed vegetables and two plain.

The prices of vegetables average as follows: artichokes, from 2s. 6d. to 6s. 6d. per doz.; cauliflower, from 3s. 6d. to 6s. 6d. per doz.; French beans, from 6d. to 8d. per lb.; mushrooms, from 1s. 6d. to 2s. 6d. per basket; seakale, from 2s. 6d. to 3s. 6d. per bundle; spinach, from 4d. to 6d. per lb.; asparagus, from 3s. to 10s. per hundred; peas, from 1s. 6d. to 2s. 6d. per pint; broad beans, 8d. to 10d. per lb.; cucumbers, from 1s. to 2s. each.

The following dressed vegetables are given in turn by those who make dinner giving a study:—

Tomates farcies; Chou de mer à l'Anglaise; Asperges à l'Anglaise; Macédoine de légumes; Petits Pois à l'Anglaise; Salade aux Tomates; Haricots verts sautés; Chou-fleur au gratin; Champignons grillés; Champignons au gratin; Artichants à l'Anglaise; Epinards au jus; Céleris au jus; Choux de Bruxelles sautés; Tomates au gratin; Pommes de terre frites; Pommes de terre à la Maître d'Hôtel; Truffes en serviette; Jerusalem Artichokes à la Crême.

The roast is followed by *entremets*, savory *entremets* and sweet *entremets*, but they are both classed on the *menu* under the head of *entremets*, only without any distinctive character beyond that they stand first, and are served in the order in which they stand. For a party of eighteen it is usual to give two savories and three sweets, though at a men's dinner only two of the latter would be given; for a smaller number of guests one savory and a dressed vegetable, and two sweets, would be given in addition to the dressed vegetables served with the *rôts*. The following are the best *entremets* to give at both large and small dinners. In serving *entremets*, as in *entrées* at all dinner parties numbering over ten guests, it is always advisable to have double *entremets*, as it expedites the serving of dinner, and entails no increased expense in the matter of providing the quantity required:—

Fonds d'Artichauts à l'Italienne; Huîtres au gratin; Aspic de Crevettes à la Tartare; Pâté de Foie Gras à l'Aspic; Omelette aux Tomates; Omelette aux Huîtres; Asperges glacés; Asperges en surprise; Croutes d'Oeufs de Pluviers aux tomates; Oeufs de Pluviers en Aspics; Biscuits de Crevettes; Canapés de Crevettes; Crevettes en Croustade; Canapés d'Anchois.

The cost of either Fonds d'Artichauts à l'Italienne, Huîtres au gratin, Aspic de Crevettes à la Tartare, and Pâté de Foie Gras à l'Aspic for a party of eighteen, would average from 8s. to 10s.

The cost of Omelette aux Huîtres for this number of people

would average from 8s. to 10s. and Omelette aux Tomates, 5s. to 6s.

The cost of Asperges glacés, or Asperges en surprise, depends upon the season of the year, and would average from 5s. to 15s. for a party of eighteen.

The same remark applies to plovers' eggs, which range from 3s. to 8s. per doz. For a party of eighteen, 2½ to 3 doz. would be the proportion.

The cost of either Biscuits de Crevettes, Canapés de Crevettes, and Crevettes en Croustade, for a party of eighteen, would amount to from 6s. to 7s.

Beignets de Parmesan; Iced Soufflé au Parmesan; Fondu au Parmesan; Petits Soufflés au Fromage; Petites Coquilles de Macaroni au gratin; Macaroni au gratin. Any of the *entremets* of cheese for the before-mentioned number of guests would cost from 3s. to 4s.

In providing sweet *entremets* for a party of eighteen, two or three would be given; and for a party of eight, two would still be given, one not offering sufficient choice. The cost of any of the following jellies for a party of eighteen would average from 5s. to 7s., according to the jelly selected:—

Gelée à l'Ananas; Gelée au Kirsch Ganie de Cerises; Gelée d'Oranges; Gelée de Pêches au Noyeau; Gelée au Maraschino; Macédoine Gelée.

The cost of any of the creams here given would average for a party of eighteen from 5s. to 7s.

Crême au Caramel; Crême à l'Italienne, Crême de Fraises; Crême d'Ananas; Crême de Mille Fruits; Crême de Vanille; Crême de Pêches.

Gateau de compote d'Abricots aux Framboises; Beignots d'Abricots; Pain d'Abricot; Chartreuse d'Abricot; Omelette d'Abricot.

Either of those *entremets* of apricots would average 8s. for a party of eighteen.

The following *entremets* would average the same:—

Pudding à l'Ananas; Plombières glacés; Pudding glacé à la

Nesselrode; Bombe glacé à la Macédoine; iced pudding à la Macédoine; Purée de Groseilles glacées; Vol au vent de Fruit à la Crême glacé; Baba au compote d'Ananas; Pyramides de Fruits; Célestine de Fraises à l'Anglaise; Macédoine de Fruits; Suprême de Fruits.

Purée de Groseilles glacées would not amount to more than 4s. for this given number of guests.

In providing the *entremets* of fruit here given, for a party of eighteen the cost would average from 8s. to 12s., according to the season of the year and the kind of fruit chosen.

Petits Savarins au Liqueur; Soufflé glacé au Liqueur; Soufflé de Vanille glacé. The cost of either of these sweets for a party of eighteen would not exceed 6s.

The following are inexpensive sweets, and would average about 4s. to 5s.:—

Chartreuse de Pommes à la Crême; Meringues à la Crême; Petits Biscuits glacés à la Vanille; Compote de marrons aux Oranges.

At large dinner parties the *entremets* are followed by two *relevés* belonging to the order of piquant savories. At small dinner parties but one of these savory *relevés* are given. The following are the most generally liked, the cost of which for a party of eighteen would average 4s. to 5s., according to the one selected. *Relevés* composed of caviare or anchovy are sometimes given at the commencement of dinner before oysters or soup, and are then styled *Hors d'Oeuvres*.

Canapés de Jambon; Canapés de Homard; Petits Bouchées à l'Indienne; Sandwiches de Parmesan; Croûtes de Caviare; Croûtes à la Marinière; Croûtes de Jambon au Parmesan; Croûtes de Jambon à la Madras; Croûtes au Parmesan; Croûtes of Anchovy; Canapés of Bloater; Croûtes de Laitances; Pailles de Parmesan; Favorites à la Royale; Favorites à la Duchesse; Biscuit de Fromage; Petits Filets de Saumon au Diable.

The ices usually given at dinner parties include the following:—
Abricot à l'Eau; L'eau d'Ananas; L'eau de Cerises; L'eau de Tangerine; Vanille à la Crême; Crême de Fraises; Crême du Pain

Mes. Water ice can be made at home at 2s. per quart, and cream ice at 4s. per quart.

In providing ices it is usual to give one water ice and one cream ice; the proportion would be one pint to every eight dinner guests.

The dessert is with many an expensive feature. The cost of fruit for dessert also depends upon the season of the year and upon the fruit selected. As a rule the dinner governs the fruit; if a smart and expensive dinner were given, a smart and expensive dessert would follow; if an inexpensive dinner provided, the dessert would be given on the same scale.

For a party of eighteen, eight dishes of fruit would be the proportion.

The quantity of wine drunk at dinner parties varies so considerably, that it is difficult to lay down any hard or fast rule as to the number of bottles a given number of guests would actually drink. Thus with regard to champagne, one man would drink from three-quarters of a bottle to a bottle, another would drink say two glasses, while a third would confine himself to claret and decline champagne altogether.

In providing champagne, half a bottle to each man and a third of a bottle to each lady would be a fair proportion. 84s. per dozen is an average price to give for champagne, but in many cases and in many places champagne worth 60s. per dozen is charged at 84s. or champagne worth 84s. is charged at 96s. per dozen. Therefore a certain amount of experience and knowledge of the quality of wines in general is necessary when selecting them, to avoid paying a high price for an inferior wine.

Sherry is but little drunk at dinner parties, and is only handed once during dinner, that is after soup, and once at dessert. Sherry at 48s. per dozen is considered a fair price to give, while sherry at 72s. is a price but seldom exceeded.

When claret is preferred to champagne by a guest, a sound dinner claret at about 74s. per dozen is provided. Good judges of claret would give from 12s. 6d. to a guinea per bottle for a favourite vintage; but the generality of hosts are content to pay 96s. per dozen for after-dinner claret. For a party of eighteen, four bottles of after-dinner claret would be an average proportion, and two bottles of sherry.

Port wine and Madeira are but seldom given, unless they are very choice of their kind, and have been in the cellars some thirty or forty years.

When light wines are given in the fish course, Hock, Chablis, or Sauterne, the price averages that of sherry, unless they too are very rare or self-imported.

The cost of floral decorations for a dinner table greatly depends upon the season of the year, that is to say, in the summer month a handsome display of flowers might be compassed at but a small expense, whilst in the winter months a good show of flowers on at dinner table would amount to something considerable.

In selecting flowers for a dinner table those possessing very powerful odours should be avoided, such as hyacinths, cape jassmine, syringa, etc., etc., and the preference given to those flowers which have a refreshing rather than a faint, heavy perfume, as in a dining-room of small dimensions guests often feel a sense of oppression from this cause, by which the appetite suffers and the relish for the good dinner provided destroyed. Colour and contrast are a great point to be considered in the choice of flowers for a dinner party, and light foliage to heavy foliage, cut blooms to flowering plants.

The cost of cut blooms varies from 1s. to 12s. per dozen, and the quantity of flowers required must be regulated according to the size of the dinner table and the extent of decoration intended.

XII

THINGS IN SEASON

A TABLE OF THINGS IN season is here given by way of offering some assistance in the arrangement of a *menu*, whether for a breakfast, luncheon, or ball-supper. The commoner kinds of fish and strictly household vegetables, herbs, &c., have not been included in the list, as it is not necessary to mention them in a work of this character.

A thing first in season is at all times most appreciated, and is then esteemed little short of a delicacy, but when the palate has become accustomed to it, if not satiated by it, it is no longer eaten with relish or zest, if eaten at all. An experienced hostess does not prolong the appearance of either fish, flesh, or fowl up to this point, but is constantly on the look-out for something new in its season wherewith to replace the waning favourites. Ignorance of when things are in season often causes a hostess to overlook something that has just come in, in favour of something that is just going out, and although inquiries can of course be made of a fishmonger, poulterer, butcher, greengrocer, or fruiterer, as to what is in season and what is to be had, yet such inquiries, whether made by the cook or by the mistress, entail loss of time, and occasion no little trouble if not mistakes, besides arguing a want of knowledge on the part of a customer, of which advantage is not unlikely to be taken by those tradesmen less scrupulous than their fellows.

JANUARY

Fish

Salmon	Crimped Cod	Turbot	Soles
Whiting	Mullet	Eels	Haddocks
Smelts	Mackerel	Lobsters	Crabs
Oysters	Prawns	Crawfish	

Poultry and Game

Turkeys	Geese	Fowls	Pigeons
Ducks	Ducklings	Guinea Fowls	Larks
Capons	Pheasants	Partridges	Woodcocks
Widgeons	Snipes	Golden Plovers	Ptarmigans
Capercailzies	Wild Ducks	Teal	Prairie Hens
Quails	Hares	Rabbits	

Meat

Beef	Veal	Mutton	House Lamb

Vegetables

Asparagus (forced)	Seakale (forced)	Mushrooms (forced)	Cauliflower
Cucumbers	Artichokes	Brussels Sprouts	Lettuces
French Beans (forced)	Carrots	Turnips	Small Salad
Radishes	Rhubarb	Spinach	Celery

Fruit

Grapes	Pears	Pines	Oranges
Walnuts	Medlars	Apples	

FEBRUARY

Fish

Salmon	Trout	Whiting	Soles
Mackerel	Mullet	Turbot	Brill
Dory	Fresh Herrings	Oysters	Crabs
Lobsters	Cod	Haddock	Smelts
Eels	Gurnet		

Poultry and Game

Turkeys	Fowls	Guinea Fowls	Pigeons
Ducks	Ducklings	Goslings	Geese
Capons	Larks	Widgeons	Wild Ducks
Quails	Prairie Hens	Woodcocks	Snipe
Golden Plovers	Teal	Ptarmigan	

Meat

Beef	Mutton	Veal	House Lamb

Vegetables

Asparagus (forced)	Seakale (forced)	Spinach	Radishes
Artichokes	Brussels Sprouts	Cauliflower	Cucumbers
French Beans (forced)	Turnips	Lettuces	Carrots
Mushrooms	Celery	Small Salad	Rhubarb

Fruit

Pines	Grapes	Pears	Apples
Oranges			

MARCH

Fish

Salmon	Turbot	Cod	Trout
Soles	Whiting	Mullet	Mackerel
Eels	Fresh Herrings	Dory	Prawns
Oysters	Lobsters	Crabs	Crawfish
Gurnets			

Poultry and Game

Turkeys	Goslings	Ducks	Ducklings
Capon	Fowls	Guinea Fowls	Pigeons
Ptarmigan	Prairie Hens	Black Game	Quails

Meat

Beef	Mutton	Veal	House Lamb

Vegetables

Spinach	Parsnips	Cucumbers	French beans
Jerusalem Artichokes	Lettuces	Small Salad	Mushrooms
Rhubarb	Turnips	Celery	Radishes
Broccoli			

Fruit

Pines	Strawberries (forced)	Pears	Apples

APRIL

Fish

Salmon	Trout	Turbot	Cod
Brill	Soles	Mullets	Smelts
Eels	Fresh Herrings	Lobsters	Crabs
Oysters	Prawns		

Poultry and Game

Goslings	Ducks	Ducklings	Fowls
Guinea Fowls	Pigeons	Quails	Plovers' Eggs
Black Game	Ptarmigan	Leverets	

Meat

Beef	Mutton	Veal	Lamb

Vegetables

Asparagus	Peas	French Beans	Mushrooms
Spinach	Cauliflower	Sprouts	Lettuces
Celery	New Potatoes	Radishes	Small Salad

Fruit

Strawberries (forced)	Cherries (forced)	Apricots (forced)	Pears

---

MAY

Fish

Salmon	Turbot	Trout	Cod
Smelts	Mullets	Mackerel	Soles
Eels	Whitebait	Lobsters	Crabs
Prawns			

Poultry and Game

Goslings	Ducks	Ducklings	Capons
Fowls	Guinea Fowls	Pigeons	Quails
Plovers	Plovers' Eggs	Leverets	

Meat

| Beef | Mutton | Veal | Lamb |

Vegetables

Asparagus	Peas	French Beans	Broad Beans
Spinach	Cauliflower	Turnips	Carrots
Mushrooms	Cucumbers	Lettuces	Small Salad

Fruit

| Strawberries | Pineapples | Apricots | Grapes |
| Cherries | Gooseberries | Currants | Melons |

JUNE

Fish

Salmon	Trout	Mackerel	Whitebait
Turbot	Soles	Brill	Red Mullets
Lobsters	Prawns		

Poultry and Game

Turkey Poults	Goslings	Ducks	Ducklings
Fowls	Guinea Fowls	Pea Fowls	Quails
Pigeons	Plovers	Buck Venison	Leverets

Meat

Beef	Mutton	Veal	Lamb

Vegetables

Asparagus	Peas	French Beans	Broad Beans
Spinach	Cauliflower	Turnips	Carrots
Cucumbers	Mushrooms	Lettuces	Small Salad

Fruit

Pineapples	Nectarines	Peaches	Apricots
Melons	Grapes	Strawberries	Cherries
Raspberries	Currants	Gooseberries	

JULY

Fish

Salmon	Trout	Mackerel	Whitebait
Turbot	Soles	Brill	Red Mullet
Lobsters	Prawns		

Poultry and Game

Turkey Poults	Goslings	Ducks	Ducklings
Fowls	Pigeons	Buck Venison	Leverets

Meat

Beef	Mutton	Veal	Lamb

Vegetables

Peas	French Beans	Broad Beans	Cauliflower
Cucumbers	Mushrooms	Lettuces	Small Salad

Fruit

Pineapples	Nectarines	Peaches	Apricots
Melons	Grapes	Strawberries	Cherries
Raspberries	Currants	Gooseberries	Plums

AUGUST

Fish

Salmon	Trout	Cod	Turbot
Soles	Brill	Mackerel	Mullet
Oysters	Lobsters	Prawns	

Poultry and Game

Turkey Poults	Goslings	Ducks	Ducklings
Fowls	Pigeons	Grouse	Black Game
Buck Venison	Leverets		

Meat

Beef	Mutton	Veal	Lamb

Vegetables

Peas	French Beans	Broad Beans	Cauliflower
Cucumber	Mushrooms	Lettuces	Small Salad

Fruit

Melon	Green Figs	Peaches	Nectarines
Apricots	Pears	Grapes	Mulberries
Currants	Gooseberries	Plums	Cherries

SEPTEMBER

Fish

Salmon	Turbot	Brill	Mackerel
Mullet	Whiting	Soles	Eels
Oysters	Lobsters	Crabs	

Poultry and Game

Turkey Poults	Geese	Ducks	Ducklings
Fowls	Partridges	Grouse	Buck Venison
Hares	Teal	Larks	

Meat

Beef	Mutton	Veal	Lamb

Vegetables

French Beans	Peas	Artichokes	Cauliflower
Spinach	Cucumbers	Mushrooms	Salad

Fruit

Pineapples	Figs	Grapes	Melons
Plums	Currants	Cherries	Quinces

OCTOBER

Fish

Salmon (Dutch)	Turbot	Cod	Brill
Mackerel	Whiting	Soles	Eels
Oysters	Lobsters		

Poultry and Game

Turkeys	Geese	Ducks	Fowls
Pheasants	Partridges	Grouse	Widgeon
Wild Duck	Teal	Venison	Hares

Meat

Beef	Mutton	Veal	Lamb

Vegetables

French Beans	Artichokes	Cauliflower	Salad
Cucumbers	Mushrooms		

Fruit

Pineapples	Grapes	Figs	Pears
Peaches	Apples	Quinces	Filberts

NOVEMBER

Fish

Salmon	Turbot	Brill	Dory
Cod	Soles	Eels	Smelts
Lobsters	Oysters		

Poultry and Game

Turkeys	Geese	Ducks	Fowls
Pheasants	Partridges	Black Game	Widgeon
Wild Ducks	Woodcock	Golden Plovers	Teal
Ptarmigan	Larks	Snipes	Venison

Meat

Beef	Mutton	Veal	Lamb

Vegetables

French Beans	Spinach	Artichokes	Cauliflower
Mushrooms	Cucumbers	Lettuces	Salad

Fruit

Pineapple	Grapes	Figs	Pears
Apples	Medlars	Filberts	

DECEMBER

Fish

Salmon	Turbot	Briıı	Dory
Soles	Cod	Red Mullet	Smelts
Oysters	Lobsters		

Poultry and Game

Turkeys	Geese	Ducks	Fowls
Pheasants	Partridges	Grouse	Wild Ducks
Widgeon	Capercailzie	Ptarmigan	Doe Venison
Teal	Larks	Hares	Golden Plovers

Meat

Beef	Mutton	Veal	Lamb

Vegetables

Asparagus (forced)	Seakale	Artichokes	Cauliflower
Spinach	French Beans	Cucumbers	Mushrooms
Rhubarb	Lettuces	Salad	

Fruit

Pineapples	Grapes	Pears	Oranges
Walnuts	Filberts		

Also available from Nonsuch Publishing

For forthcoming titles and sales information see
www.nonsuch-publishing.com